DOUBLE BILL

Alan Mullery, MBE, joined Fulham as a 15 year old in the 1950s and went on to captain Fulham, Tottenham and England. He made the journey across London to join Tottenham in 1964 and went on to make 373 appearances for the North London giants. Along the way, he scored 30 goals. He was voted 'Man of the Match' in the 1967 FA Cup final when Spurs beat Chelsea 2–1 and, as captain, led the team to the 1971 League Cup and also the 1972 UEFA Cup. He was awarded 35 England caps and played in the 1970 World Cup finals in Mexico, where England were the defending champions. In 1972, he returned to Fulham and was a member of the team which lost the 1975 FA Cup final to West Ham. In the same year, he was voted 'Player of the Year'. Success in management quickly followed and he led Brighton & Hove Albion into the old First Division. He followed this with a media career which included an acclaimed radio phone-in show for London's Capital Gold Sport. He is now seen regularly as a football pundit on Sky Sports TV. He lives in West Sussex with his wife, June.

Paul Trevillion, CGLI Full Tech, has been acclaimed as the finest sports artist Europe has ever produced. Born in Love Lane, only two minutes from the Spurs ground, he went to the St Francis de Sales School opposite the Tottenham football ground but could not read or write until he was 13 years old. He spent most of his school days missing lessons to stand outside the Spurs ground collecting autographs, along with a caning from his headmaster on his return. In 1952, Paul received a letter from Buckingham Palace in which His Royal Highness, The Duke of Edinburgh, called the portrait Paul had drawn of him 'a very good piece of work'.

The story was published in the *Tottenham Weekly Herald* and *Lilywhite*, the journal of the Spurs Supporters Club, which then went on to publish Paul's Spurs cartoons and caricatures. Paul is the author and illustrator of over 20 sports books that have sold worldwide, including Peter Alliss's *Easier Golf*, which was reprinted 10 times. He also illustrated *Gary Player's Golf Class*, which appeared in over 300 newspapers worldwide – the largest syndicated sports feature in the world. In more recent years, Paul illustrated skill books by Spurs legends Gary Lineker and Paul Gascoigne. He is both humble and proud that a collection of his Spurs work is housed in Tottenham's famous Bruce Castle Museum. Paul lives in Bedfordshire with his wife, Lorraine, and the youngest two of his five sons, Luke and John.

DOUBLE BILL

The Bill Nicholson Story

Alan Mullery
and **Paul Trevillion**

Foreword by Eddie Baily

MAINSTREAM
PUBLISHING

EDINBURGH AND LONDON

First published in Great Britain in 2005 by
MAINSTREAM PUBLISHING COMPANY
(EDINBURGH) LTD
7 Albany Street
Edinburgh EH1 3UG

ISBN 1 84596 002 5

A catalogue record for this book
is available from the British Library

Typeset in Ellington and Frutiger

Printed and bound in Great Britain by
William Clowes Ltd, Beccles, Suffolk

To June, my wife – a tower of strength at all times.
Alan Mullery

To my three grown-up sons, Mark (Tottenham's no. 1 fan), Steven (boxing authority) and Christopher (Karate 3rd Dan).
Paul Trevillion

AND HERE'S HOPING . . .

In This Issue -

★ **Highlights of 1951-52**
In Pictures

★ **Enrolments**
G. K. Long

★ **My Greatest Game**
Ted Ditchburn

★ **Pass It On**
A. G. Franklin

★ **Spiers of the Spurs**
Les Yates

**Cartoons and Drawings
throughout by
PAUL TREVILLION**

THE DUKE HONOURS OUR CARTOONIST

H.R.H. The Duke of Edinburgh has accepted a cartoon of himself drawn by PAUL TREVILLION.

We hope this portends a successful future for our talented young contributor.

Lilywhite magazine, 1952

Acknowledgements

The authors would like to thank Peter Willis for his meticulous research and his tireless and inspirational assistance in the putting-together of this book. Also, special thanks goes to June Mullery, Lorraine Trevillion, Bill Campbell, Graeme Blaikie, Kevin O'Brien and all at Mainstream Publishing.

Contents

Foreword

While I am highly honoured to write this foreword, it would be hypocritical for me to say that everything was sweetness and light between me and Bill *all* the time – it wasn't. But I believe every successful partnership is made up of two opposites: that's why they work, and in our partnership the chemistry worked very well.

Bill was your typical no-nonsense dour Yorkshireman and I was the cheeky, cocky cockney. Put the two together and you had a winning partnership.

I probably featured in Bill's legendary history-making life down at Tottenham more than most people. I knew Bill for ten years as a player and I worked with him for twelve years as his assistant-manager and coach. That's twenty-two years.

We were teammates in the 'push-and-run' Spurs side managed by Arthur Rowe in the '50s which won the Second Division and First Division titles in successive seasons. As a player back in those days, Bill was what I would call a very hard-working, very reliable teammate. He may not have been the most skilful, but nobody demanded more of themselves on the field. When he became a manager, the workload he expected of his players was only a fraction of the demands he had placed upon himself. Even back then, Bill was very serious-minded and very eager and keen to learn about the game. He was always immaculately dressed and he never put a foot wrong. He was a credit to Tottenham.

I worked alongside Bill again from 1962 to 1974, this time as his assistant-manager, and between us we guided Spurs to more glory following Bill's historic Double success of 1961. Bill had a prodigious appetite for hard work and his planning as a manager was meticulous: nothing was left to chance. Bill and I managed to find a successful way forward which best suited the players we had at Tottenham. We wanted Spurs to be breathtaking in style and skill and win in a manner that entertained and electrified the crowd. Spurs thrived in cup competitions and over the years we and the players added new silverware to the Tottenham trophy cabinet.

Bill treated all of us at Tottenham with great respect. He was a man of great integrity, who never once made a promise he didn't keep.

I am immensely proud of what Bill and I achieved and won together at Tottenham both as players in the '50s and later as a management team. It was a truly wonderful partnership – one I will never forget.

Eddie Baily

Lilywhite magazine, 1952

Preface

When Bill Nicholson died on 23 October 2004, a light certainly went out in my life. When I joined Tottenham in 1964, I entered a new world of football – Bill Nicholson's world. 'Don't call me boss – my name's Bill,' was his first instruction and that set the tone for a very fruitful relationship which led me to becoming captain of Spurs with the privilege of working closely with the great man.

In this book, I have tried to give the reader an insight into the real Bill Nicholson – the Bill Nicholson who loved and nurtured his players, set their performance benchmarks high and inspired them to play well above themselves. As you will read, Bill tended to be a man of few words – he let his team do all the talking on the pitch.

None talked better than Bill's never-to-be-forgotten Double-winning side of 1961. They produced near perfect football and for Bill, the ultimate perfectionist, that must have been very sweet music indeed.

I was honoured to be asked by Mainstream Publishing to write this book on Bill – a man who played such a big role in my career and whom I had the utmost respect for. He was indeed a decent, loyal man: a man who should have been knighted for his services to football while he was still with us. Maybe, if enough of us make a loud enough noise, it's still not too late. A posthumous knighthood for Bill would be richly deserved and, in this book, both myself and my co-author Paul

Trevillion urge readers to get behind the campaign to make it Sir Bill Nicholson.

Despite his total devotion to football, Bill was a family man and his wife Grace – or Darkie as she was known to most – plus daughters Jean and Linda, must have been very proud of Bill. They had every reason to be.

Bill has deserved all the accolades which have come his way since October 2004. I hope my memories of a wonderful football man enrich the tributes in a unique, honest and revealing way.

Alan Mullery

* * *

Bill Nicholson's Double-winning team guaranteed him a special place in the hearts of all Spurs fans. His unprecedented achievements as the Tottenham manager set the template by which successors are judged. But it must never be forgotten that Bill had a very successful career as a player at Spurs before entering the manager's office.

As a lifelong Spurs fan, I was fortunate enough in my schoolboy days to watch the famous Arthur Rowe Tottenham push-and-run team. (I saw my first-ever Spurs game at the age of two and a half and then, from the age of three, I never missed a Spurs home game for the next 30 years; it was even reported in the *Tottenham Weekly Herald* that I came back early from my honeymoon to watch Spurs play their home game against West Ham.) I would stand for hours outside White Hart Lane with my autograph book open, pen in hand, desperate to get the team's signatures, and the very first one I got was signed 'W. Nicholson'.

I could draw before I could walk – a pencil was never out of my hand – and I drew Bill and all the Tottenham players in those early days and I would ask them to sign the sketch. My drawings of the Spurs players were published in the *Tottenham Weekly Herald* and Spurs' *Lilywhite* magazine and on many occasions my drawings featured Nicholson.

Over the years, I have stored away many of those early published Tottenham illustrations and some are reproduced in the pages of this book, along with my cherished memories of Bill.

In later years, my relationship with Bill was, in the main, linked to my work as a writer and illustrator on the sports pages of the *Sunday Times* and *Sunday People*. At all times when I spoke to Bill, I found him very brief, but also very helpful, and over the years we developed an understanding of just how far each of us would go in our professional relationship of newspaper journalist and manager.

It goes without saying that, as a die-hard Spurs supporter, I loved the man. He was responsible for the greatest sporting memories of my life.

Bill was a great player, a great manager, but he was an even greater human being.

Paul Trevillion

Tottenham Weekly Herald, 1961

CHAPTER ONE

From Scarborough to Spurs

The daunting, towering benchmark which Bill Nicholson had to aspire to when he became the Tottenham Hotspur manager had been firmly set in place by the team in which he played – the record-breaking Arthur Rowe push-and-run side that perfected a quick-passing, skilful, attacking game and won the Second and First Division Championships in successive seasons.

Bill Nicholson was a very private man, not one who would sit down and talk to you about his early days, but when you wore the Spurs shirt for as long as I did, it was possible to garner together enough knowledge to make me feel I really knew the man.

William Edward Nicholson was born in Scarborough on 26 January 1919, one of five brothers and four sisters. Bill's father worked with horses for a Hansom cab company and from a young age Bill helped out, but he never learned to ride a horse. Just as surprisingly, even though he lived close to one of the finest beaches on the Scarborough coast, he never learned to swim.

I well remember one end of season when Spurs were on holiday in Spain and Bill for the first time came near the hotel swimming pool. At no time had he been in the pool, so some of the players surrounded Bill and tried to throw him, fully clothed, into the water. It was at that moment that I realised just how strong Bill was. No matter how hard the lads tried, they couldn't push him over the edge into the pool. They had to admit defeat and give up. I thought that was the last we'd see of him as he disappeared off, but I was wrong. He came back. He had gone away to change into a lightweight shirt and a pair of shorts and this time, when the boys again charged in, Bill didn't put up a fight; he let the players throw him in. They all enjoyed the joke and I also noticed Bill had made sure it was the shallow end!

At the age of seven, young Bill was given a rubber ball and with his first kick his destiny was decided. From kickabouts with the local children, he went on to play centre-half in the school team at the Scarborough Boys High School. Bill told me he liked playing at centre-half – that's the position he played when he first got into the Spurs team – but although he was good in the air, he reckoned he was just a little bit on the short side for that position. I believe that was why Bill, as a manager, always played a 6-ft-plus centre-half in the Spurs defence: players like Maurice Norman and Mike England.

Bill never played for any schoolboy representative team, so he was not spotted by any of the Football League scouts. When he left school at 16, he got a job in a laundry. Bill played his football for the Young Liberals side in the local Scarborough League. The manager, who was also the town dentist, had words with Tottenham's York-based scout and he arranged for Bill to be invited to Spurs for a month's trial. Apparently, up until that point, Bill's mother and father had never once seen him play. I find this amazing, but not totally surprising because Bill was a very modest man who wouldn't have gone around shouting from the rooftops to his family about his footballing skills.

Bill did well enough down at Tottenham to be taken on as a ground-staff boy at £2 per week. Bill did talk about that time. He would tell you he worked hard – and he would emphasise *hard* – from 8 a.m. until 5 p.m. every weekday. Bill reckoned at one time he must have painted every square inch of the Tottenham ground, and when he wasn't painting, he was working on the pitch. Bill played very little football.

Training was twice a week, which was, in the main, a lot of running, but Bill reckoned running was a lot better than painting. Bill told me he enjoyed the training and all the running and that stayed with him all his life. No matter how many hours Bill spent with the lads when I was at Tottenham, his inexhaustible enthusiasm for training never let up – he would train us, train us and train us. He never liked calling a break or having to call an end to it.

Bill signed as a full-time Tottenham professional aged 18, on the same day as his good friend Ron Burgess. In all my time with Bill, he rarely praised and never went overboard when talking about the ability of great players – and we did have some great players at Tottenham – but Burgess was the exception. He was Bill's – as he would often repeat – favourite player in the days when the two of them were in the Spurs push-and-run team. Ron Burgess was the yardstick that Bill would go on to measure all his midfield players by, and that included Blanchflower and Mackay. Burgess was, and Bill never tired of telling this to anyone who would listen, the perfect player. He had the lot: good in the air, two good feet, a ball-winner, an excellent passer, scored goals and, on top of all that, he never stopped running. Not surprisingly, the first player Bill picked in his 'best ever' Tottenham team, selected from the footballers he had played with and managed, was Ron Burgess. The two of them played a few games in the First Team but, with the outbreak of the Second World War in 1939, it all came to an end.

Bill joined the Durham Light Infantry, rising to the rank of sergeant, working as an instructor first in infantry training – soldiers who fight on foot – moving on to work with the troops as a PE instructor. Having been worked over by Bill with the rest of the lads at the Spurs training ground, I can imagine how hard Bill worked those soldiers. It goes without saying: Bill would have had the fittest troops in the Army!

After the war and back at Spurs in 1946, Bill went straight into the Tottenham first team at centre-half. He also attended the FA coaching course at Birmingham University and passed his full badge at the first attempt. Bill never hid the fact that he enjoyed those six and a half years in the Army, training and instructing the troops. I have no doubt that those Army days decided his future. That's why, when he came out of the Army, he wasted no time in getting his FA coaching badge. Bill knew, when he hung up his boots, he could continue working with men as a football coach and, of course, Bill did just that – complete with Army discipline and his trademark sergeant-major's haircut.

By 1948, Bill had established himself as the regular Tottenham right-half. He was an untiring, hard-working, ball-winning defender who rarely gave the ball away. He played a vital part in the legendary Arthur Rowe Spurs side that destroyed the opposition. The Tottenham fans loved this entertaining style of football and Nicholson, to his credit, never forgot this. Every team Bill managed from those days on had to play with style – had to entertain the fans – and he would settle for nothing less. Fall below that standard and Bill would give you a very hard time in the dressing-room after the match – and it didn't even matter if you'd won.

Bill got just the one England cap and scored with his first kick against Portugal at Everton's Goodison Park ground, although he was selected as an England reserve on 22 occasions, which I believe is a record!

* * *

The 1954–55 season saw Bill end his playing days, as did his great friend, Ron Burgess. My co-author Paul Trevillion recalls that time:

I had the great honour, when the Tottenham immortal Ron Burgess said goodbye, of my drawing of Burgess appearing on the front cover of the Spurs *Lilywhite* magazine, accompanying Ron's farewell message to the fans.

I well remember, before I sent the drawing to the *Lilywhite*, I showed it to Ron Burgess, who at the time was standing outside the Spurs ground talking to Bill Nicholson.

'It's an excellent likeness,' said Burgess, who was always very kind and complimentary. 'Here, Bill,' he said, handing it to Nicholson. 'What do you think?'

Nicholson took a look at the drawing and came straight back: 'You could have been drawn with a little bit more hair, Ron.'

Without thinking, I chipped in, 'If you, Bill, had a little bit more skill, you could have been another Ron Burgess.'

It was an unnecessary remark which wasn't even funny. I wished the ground could have swallowed me up and Bill snapped back, 'A *bit* more skill? It would have taken a LOT. This man . . .' and with that he pointed at Burgess, 'is the finest player to ever wear a Spurs shirt. In all your lifetime, you'll never see a better player. You've been very privileged to watch him play!'

As Nicholson and Burgess began to walk off, Ron turned and said, 'Bill's much too hard on himself. He's the cornerstone of the Tottenham defence.'

I've always believed that the Ron Burgess *Lilywhite* 'Goodbye!' spoke for both men and I am pleased Alan Mullery agreed it should be reproduced in full. It shows just how close and how important the Tottenham fans were to those Spurs players in the famous push-and-run days. This is an affinity which Nicholson never, ever lost.

The *Lilywhite*: September 1954

Ron Burgess Says 'Good-bye!'

It is only natural, I suppose, that I should feel some regret at leaving Tottenham, where I have had my roots for so long. It was in May 1936, as a lad of 17, that I left South Wales to join Spurs' junior side, with a burning ambition to succeed in big-time football.

That I have achieved my ambition in some measure gives me real pleasure, and I think I can say that I owe it all to Tottenham. It hasn't always been easy, of course. I have had my disappointments, but have been most fortunate that the game has rewarded me with its highest honours, all of them gained whilst wearing Spurs' white shirt.

That fact fills me with pride, for I have been privileged to play for one of the greatest clubs in the land, and I have no regrets whatever that I threw in my football with Spurs 18 years ago.

Life has been good to me at Tottenham. I have made many, many friends whom I am sorry to leave – friends within the club and amongst the supporters: all of whom have been very good to me during all my years at Tottenham. I have been frankly amazed at the number of comparative strangers who have stopped me recently and expressed their regret at my departure to Swansea. I could ask for no greater appreciation of my efforts on the field.

I want to express my sincere gratitude to every one of you for giving me such encouragement and support. I shall never forget the happy times I have spent with you all.

And now that the time for farewell has come, I ask you to carry on your good work on behalf of the Spurs, and to continue to show your appreciation of the younger players who will wear the colours of the club in the future.

Very best wishes to all.

RON BURGESS

* * *

Alan Mullery continues:

Nicholson took over a coaching role at Tottenham when he retired from playing in 1955. Arthur Rowe left the club through ill health shortly afterwards, and Jimmy Anderson became the manager.

Anderson immediately set about rebuilding the push-and-run side and he signed three players: Bobby Smith, Maurice Norman and Cliff Jones. They made a big impact, but not enough to win trophies during the three years Anderson was manager. Meanwhile, Nicholson was busy and not only at Tottenham. He went to Sweden and was a big success when he coached the England World Cup team in the 1958 World Cup finals. He wasn't back at Tottenham long when Jimmy Anderson left. Nicholson was appointed manager, and on the same day Spurs thrashed Everton by 10–4.

Nicholson then continued the rebuilding work. He signed three Scotsmen: Dave Mackay, Bill Brown and John White. He also made the short trip to Chelsea and swapped Johnny Brooks for Les Allen. Nicholson had now made Spurs a formidable and much-feared side.

Under the captaincy of Danny Blanchflower, the 1960–61 season started with Tottenham winning their first 11 games. Manchester City were the first side to take a point from White Hart Lane. Tottenham went on to play 16 games before their first defeat, at Sheffield Wednesday, and the season ended with the historic Double. They were the first team to achieve this feat since Aston Villa in 1897.

Blanchflower summed it all up when he said, 'The Tottenham Double team played an exciting, attacking, entertaining style of

SEPTEMBER, 1954

THE *Lilywhite*

THE OFFICIAL ORGAN OF THE SPURS SUPPORTERS CLUB

Vol. 5 No. 1   *Affiliated to the National Federation of Supporters Clubs*   Price **6d.**

Ron Burgess

says "Good-bye!"

*I*T is only natural, I suppose, that I should feel some regret at leaving Tottenham where I have had my roots for so long. It was in May 1936, as a lad of 17, that I left South Wales to join Spurs' Junior side, with a burning ambition to succeed in big-time football.

That I have achieved my ambition in some measure gives me real pleasure, and I think I can say that I owe it all to Tottenham. It hasn't always been easy, of course. I have had my disappointments, but have been most fortunate that the game has rewarded me with its highest honours, all of them gained whilst wearing Spurs' white shirt.

That fact fills me with pride, for I have been privileged to play for one of the greatest clubs in the land, and I have no regrets whatever that I threw in my football with Spurs 18 years ago.

Life has been good to me at Tottenham. I have made many, many friends whom I am sorry to leave—friends within the Club and amongst the Supporters; all of whom have been very good to me during all my years at Tottenham. I have been frankly amazed at the number of comparative strangers who have stopped me recently and expressed their regret at my departure to Swansea. I could ask for no greater appreciation of my efforts on the field.

I want to express my sincere gratitude to every one of you for giving me such encouragement and support. I shall never forget the happy times I have spent with you all.

And now that the time for farewell has come, I ask you to carry on your good work on behalf of the Spurs, and to continue to show your appreciation of the younger players who will wear the colours of the Club in the future.

Very best wishes to all.

RON BURGESS.

football that will never be repeated. It was the end of an era, because it was the end of when individual players were allowed to do things their own way, thrill crowds with their individual brilliance and win in style.'

Bill's Double-winning side retained the FA Cup in 1962 and then went on to demolish Atletico Madrid 5–1 in the 1963 European Cup-Winners' Cup final, and lift the first European trophy to come to a British club.

When I joined Tottenham in 1964, Nicholson was breaking up his legendary Double-winning side and he promised me Spurs would win back the FA Cup by 1967. Bill kept his word: Tottenham won their third FA Cup in seven years by beating Chelsea 2–1 in the very first all-London Wembley final, and I had a winner's medal.

Bill delivered more besides: the League Cup in 1971 and the UEFA Cup in 1972, when I scored the winning goal in the second leg against Wolverhampton Wanderers and Tottenham became the first team to win two different European competitions.

When I left Tottenham after our UEFA Cup success, I realised that through all the severity that Bill conveyed as manager – and he was a very tough taskmaster – I had got to like the man. He was very loyal, very sincere and totally honest. Bill always demanded we won in style and insisted the fans came first. But my lasting memory is of just how tough and fit Bill was, and he had to be to carry the 24-hour workload that he demanded of himself during my time at Tottenham.

I will give you some idea of just how strong he was. When Spurs played Olympique Lyonnais in the European Cup-Winners' Cup in France, in a game which they called the Battle of Lyon, I was sent off with the French forward Andre Guy after an explosive, bloody clash. At half-time, Guy then went to attack Gilzean, and Nicholson stepped in and Guy leaped on Bill's back. I had been on the pitch playing against this fellow, Guy. He was the ultimate hard man – a real tough nut – and yet Bill simply shrugged his shoulders and flicked him off. I was amazed, and Bill, unmoved, just carried on as normal!

Bill continued to collect the silverware, winning the League Cup again in 1973. Tottenham beat Norwich 1–0. Ralph Coates scored the goal. But that sadly proved to be Bill's last trophy.

In 1974, Bill announced his retirement as the Tottenham manager.

He left and later joined up with Ron Greenwood at West Ham on the scouting staff.

Bill received his first personal honour in recognition of his services to football in 1975 when he went to Buckingham Palace to receive the OBE from the Queen Mother. In the same year, I was voted the 'Player of the Year' and received my MBE. I don't know whom I was most pleased for – Bill or myself.

When Bill's successor, Terry Neill, was replaced by Keith Burkinshaw in 1976, Keith immediately won the gratitude of every Spurs fan by bringing Bill back to White Hart Lane as a consultant and chief scout. I phoned Bill and wished him the best. I told him I was delighted he was back home.

Further recognition of Bill's lifelong devotion to football came when he was awarded the PFA Merit Award in 1984. Bill, as always, was very modest. He said he was very honoured and it came as a great surprise. Previous winners include Sir Matt Busby, Bill Shankly, Bob Paisley, Sir Tom Finney, Sir Bobby Charlton and Denis Law. Still more honours came Bill's way when in 1991 Tottenham awarded him the title of club president. Bill now held the hallowed position as the club's figurehead.

In December 1998, Bill received the Freedom of the Borough from Haringey Council and, even more appropriately, the road leading to the main entrance at White Hart Lane was renamed 'Bill Nicholson Way'.

Of one thing I am absolutely sure: there has not been one player who has worn a Tottenham shirt who has been so in love with the Tottenham club as was Bill Nicholson. It was indeed his life right up until the end, as he continued to attend every Spurs match played at White Hart Lane until shortly before his death, aged 85, on 23 October 2004.

CHAPTER TWO

My First Encounters with Bill

The first time I met Bill Nicholson I was a Fulham player and Bill was in charge of England's Under-23 side and they travelled over to Craven Cottage to play Fulham's reserves in a friendly match. It was a Tuesday morning in the late '50s. I was a young ground-staff boy at Fulham and I can remember I played out of my skin. I had a cracker of a game.

At the final whistle, Bill approached me and said, 'Son, you should be in my England team.'

Well, you can imagine how I felt. I was suddenly 10-ft tall. To get a compliment like that at my young age from Bill Nicholson, England's Under-23 manager, hit home: so much so that it is still clear in my mind today. I believed I was going to make it in professional football.

Little did I know at the time that, come 1964, I would be sitting in a room with Bill signing forms to play for his Tottenham Hotspur team. Nothing was further from my mind on that Tuesday morning at the Cottage. I was simply dreaming about playing for the Fulham first team.

But life is strange. Fast forward to March 1964 and Dave Mackay is playing for Spurs against Manchester United at Old Trafford. Mackay is involved in a 50–50 tackle with Noel Cantwell, the United defender, and he breaks his leg. At the same time, the Spurs captain Danny Blanchflower was out of the team with a cartilage operation which ended up finishing his career – medical science not being as advanced back then as it is now. Bill Nicholson had to act fast. He had lost what was then his right-half and left-half: one key defender and one midfield general in his Double-winning side of 1961.

Speculation was rife in the press as to whom Nicholson was after and Bobby Moore and myself were the two chief suspects. I wasn't restless at Fulham; I was perfectly happy with my lot at the very friendly West London club. Then one Friday night the phone rang and it was Frank Osbourne, the general manager at Fulham. It was a short conversation. He told me to drop everything, he needed to talk to me at once. It was *very* urgent. I immediately drove over to his house.

I walked into the lounge and, as I sat down, Frank immediately broke the news.

'Alan,' he said, 'Spurs have come in with an unbelievable offer for you – a British-record fee of £72,500 – and the chairman, Mr Trinder, has decided to take it.'

My first reaction was that I didn't want to go and, as I was explaining why to Frank, the doorbell rang and in walked Bill Nicholson and Eddie Baily. It was quick handshakes all round. Then we all sat down and Nicholson's first words to me were, 'Alan, can you play right-back?'

I answered immediately, 'NO – I'm a midfield player. I've always played in midfield. I'm happy in that position. I've always played in that position. I don't want to play right-back.'

Bill persisted: 'But I *need* you to play right-back. I can go and get another midfield player – but it's *you*, Alan, I want to play at right-back.'

I didn't fancy any of that, so I stood up and I said to Bill, 'No. Sorry. I'll pass.'

To his credit, Bill, who could see how strongly I felt, accepted I would not play at right-back. He relented and agreed to my way of thinking. He stood up, smiled and shook my hand.

'OK, Alan, you've made your point. I'm happy with that, so let's move forward. Play for Fulham against Liverpool tomorrow, but don't tell anyone you're going to sign for Tottenham.'

At that moment, I wasn't the happiest man. I felt I was being forced out of the club, having been told by chairman Tommy Trinder that he desperately needed the Tottenham transfer fee to improve one end of the Fulham ground. The decision was made and Nicholson, as always, had got his man. Before Nicholson left, he turned to me and said, 'As soon as tomorrow's game is over, I will meet you at your house and we'll sign the contracts.'

From then onwards, it all worked like clockwork. I played for Fulham and we beat Liverpool 1–0, which improved Spurs' position in the league and obviously pleased Nicholson. I got changed very quickly after the match, got into my car and, as I arrived home, saw Nicholson was already there waiting for me. The deal was done.

On the Monday, I drove to White Hart Lane instead of Craven Cottage. Over the weekend, Nicholson had been very busy; he had organised the lot. Even my initials were on the tracksuit he handed to me. I was a Tottenham player; Nicholson was my manager.

Quickly, very quickly, I was to learn that Nicholson's world at Tottenham was very different to life with Fulham in south-west London. I had literally no idea what to expect at Tottenham and it was to prove a real eye-opener. This, after all, was the club where three seasons earlier the Double of league championship and FA Cup had been achieved – the first time since Aston Villa in 1897. Nicholson's world was clearly inhabited by very special people with a very strict, professional attitude not found at many clubs. The place was all about results and success.

There was no big welcoming party when I drove in on my first day. I saw Bill walking across the car park. He continued to walk and I said, 'Good morning, Boss.'

Nicholson came back, 'Don't call me Boss – my name's Bill.'

I found out immediately what Bill's world at Tottenham was all about. First and foremost, Bill was obsessed by winning, and I mean *totally* obsessed. But that wasn't all: he was obsessed about winning in style.

In those days, Fulham was a relatively easygoing club. Don't get me wrong: everyone who pulled on the famous white shirt felt passionately about the club and fought like tigers to put one over on their opponents. But Bill's world at Tottenham was a real culture shock. It was a totally new environment. In blunt terms, it was a no-nonsense, hard-working, professional set-up right from the top to the very bottom. Of course, Fulham were also professional, but there was room for a laugh and a bit of fun. At Fulham, if you won it was great – we celebrated. But if you lost, it wasn't the end of the world – there was another game next week. That was the attitude at the Cottage and one of the biggest differences between the clubs.

In Bill's world at Tottenham, there was pressure to win *every* game. There were no quiet times. If it wasn't winning the league, then you were expected to be winning cups. That was the life I now faced: a ruthless, professional, hard-working existence, which had delivered glory in 1961 and was still capable of producing glory in 1964 with what was rapidly becoming a new set-up of players. There were new faces to be seen at the club almost every day, as Bill went out with his cheque book to replace the heroes of 1961.

The first thing I noticed about Bill was that he was a very quiet, modest man of very few words – until he got you in the dressing-room. Then, if he was in the mood to rip your performance in the Tottenham shirt to pieces, he would. Bill was not one to give out words of congratulation, even after a good win. He was very sparing in any words of praise. He was very demanding and a very hard man to please.

On many occasions, he would march into the dressing-room after we had won convincingly on the pitch and still give us a hard time, because we hadn't won in style and entertained the public enough! I well remember one evening game against Burnley. It had been a very hard game and we had won and all the Tottenham boys trouped into the dressing-room elated, but we were soon brought down to earth when Bill marched in. He stunned us all with a savage bout of criticism. We hadn't given the public the fast-flowing, skilful, attacking football he wanted us to play. Yes, we had won a hard game, but Bill was not pleased. We had won with a performance which in his mind had not entertained the paying customers. The public never saw that side of Bill. I am sure it would have surprised them.

But looking back now, it was that Nicholson drive for perfection which made him one of the greatest managers of all time. It produced results, because it motivated players and forced them when their legs were dead to go the extra mile in a game, and that led to trophies. At most clubs, a win was enough, but not in Bill's world.

Although Bill was very demanding on his players, amazingly

enough he was even more demanding on himself. He gave 100 per cent and then more to Spurs. It was much, much more than just a job to Bill. In those days, he would work anywhere between a 12 and 16-hour day. Apart from his coaching at the training ground at Cheshunt and the paperwork in his office, he would get in his car and travel extensively with Eddie Baily, his assistant, watching players, and if he was lucky, he got back in the early hours of the morning. Even in those days, the two of them thought nothing of flying off on a Sunday to watch foreign teams and players to check what was going on in Europe. It was very much a twenty-four hours a day, seven days a week job for Nicholson.

As I have said, Bill was a very hard man to please. Praise was a commodity in short supply. But I did get a 'pat on the back' just the once, and I remember it caused shock and disbelief in the dressing-room! I was at home on a Sunday morning and the previous day we had beaten Birmingham City. The phone rang and I answered it.

'It's Bill,' came the reply on the other end of the line. 'I just want to tell you I thought you had a good game yesterday, but in the 75th minute, in quick succession, you carelessly gave two balls away. That nearly cost us the game. I want that cut out!'

In the same breath, he put the phone down. On the Monday morning, sitting in the Tottenham dressing-room, I was changing next to Dave Mackay. I asked Dave, 'Does the manager normally call players on a Sunday?'

In his strong Scottish accent, Mackay replied, 'No. He never phones anybody!'

'Well, he called me yesterday on the phone and said I had a good game against Birmingham.'

Mackay flipped. He couldn't take it in. He stood up and shouted to the entire dressing-room, 'Bill gave Alan a phone call yesterday – to say he had a good game. Does anyone believe him?'

The entire team shook their heads, laughed and chorused at the top of their voices: 'NOOOOOOOO!!!'

Bill found it very hard to show his true emotions, especially in front of the players. No doubt inside he was pleased after a big win, but he never really showed it to us in the dressing-room.

I can remember after we had won the 1967 FA Cup final. We had beaten Chelsea in the first all-cockney final and after the game we left

Wembley and made our way to a hotel for a big reception. All the players were on a massive high and they were letting their emotions show. We occupied two tables and soon the champagne was flowing. Well, you can imagine the noise we were making. It was a mixture of very loud shouting to be heard over very loud laughter as we enjoyed ourselves and released the tension of the day. Bill was on the top table and at one point he couldn't take any more of our noisy celebration. He stood up and shouted at the top of his voice, above the din, 'You lot down there: calm down and shut up! The noise you are making is bloody awful.'

Bill sat down and we all took the hint. But at that moment I felt very sorry for Bill. He was always on duty, always the manager. He never allowed himself to be one of the boys. He never let his emotions show, even when he had a good cause. His Tottenham team had just won the FA Cup. I can honestly say that in all the years I played for Bill and captained Tottenham, I never once saw him lift up a glass of champagne to celebrate with the boys after we had won a trophy. But from what I am told, when he achieved the Double in 1961, tears were seen running down his face as the cups were paraded around Tottenham.

Nicholson's thoughts were his thoughts and his alone. No one could get inside that wise old head. Who knows, on those trophy-winning days, there may well have been one heck of a party going on in his head. I liked to think there was, because Bill deserved one.

It's possible some players may have responded to Bill better if he had openly joined in the celebrations, had a laugh and had some fun, but I wasn't one of them. I respected him for what he was and for what he had done at Tottenham. He had won plenty of silverware and I had come to Tottenham to collect medals. His track record went unchallenged. I was more than happy to accept the man on his terms. He was a workaholic who never took time off. We called him 'Bill' but he was the Boss – right round the clock and he never let you forget it for one moment.

But although Bill was a demanding boss, we liked him, because he did not rule with an iron fist when it came to off-park activities. He would treat you as a man, not as a boy, and players liked this. If you had a good game, he never minded a player having a couple of beers or more to wind down, but you didn't do your celebrating in front of Bill; you did it in private. That was why, in all my years as captain, he never once came over to me to have a moan about a player's behaviour off the pitch. Indeed, Bill's attitude was that if a player was doing it for him on the pitch, he showed no interest and didn't mind, within reason, what escapades he got up to away from the ground. Just as long as it didn't hurt the name of Tottenham Hotspur Football Club.

Bill liked his players to be married. He believed the extra responsibility would reflect in the player's performance on the pitch and in training. A settled home life with most footballers nearly always led to consistency on the park, and when I was at Tottenham it worked with the majority of the boys, although there were one or two who still liked the late night parties and clubs – it was the only way they could wind down.

Bill himself was married to Darkie and had children. I have always thought that, because he literally lived for football, he left no time for his home life and I am sure Darkie, bless her heart, had to be very understanding.

But I have to be honest: even as captain I couldn't break down the barrier and get close to Bill to have a conversation other than about football. If you went up to him and mentioned the latest goings on in *Coronation Street*, or what comedian had made you laugh, or a film you had been to see, he wouldn't have a clue what you were talking about. I suppose you would call it tunnel vision, and the only thing in Bill's tunnel was football, football and more football. I learned it was that sort of single-minded mentality that separated the men from the boys when it comes to trophy-winning success in football management.

Another thing which separated the men from the boys in the football-management jungle was attitude. Bill's attitude can be summed up in one word: WIN. If I had to name one overriding message that Bill hammered into us, it was that one word. I arrived at the club in March 1964, so my first pre-season training came in July of that year. I will never, ever forget it. On that first day, Bill ordered all 50 of us together and sat us down. His call to arms was impressive. We were reporting for duty and Bill gave us the targets for the season ahead.

'RIGHT,' he said. 'We are Tottenham Hotspur Football Club. We have got three things which we have to achieve this season: WIN the championship, WIN the FA Cup and WIN the League Cup.'

We all looked at each other, then at Bill, and thought, 'there are only three trophies out there to win – and Bill wants the lot!'

Bill, in fact, wanted to do the Treble. He left us in no doubt that he really meant what he had said. He had not said it for fun; he believed that his Tottenham team could win all three. That was his attitude and he was right to have that attitude, because three years previously he had done the Double. He had grabbed two of them, so why not all three?

This was totally new territory for me. I had never heard a battle cry like that on the first day of pre-season training before. It may have been said at Fulham, but with tongue firmly in cheek and we would all have a good laugh afterwards. But the mind-blowing thing about Bill's pronouncements was that he was deadly serious! He demanded all three trophies and he made it very clear it was our job to win them. I drove home that night knowing I had truly stepped into another world. Yes, I was in Bill's world of winning: a world which, at that time, was pure fairy-tale stuff to me.

This was the same world that was to later belong to the likes of Liverpool, Manchester United and Arsenal. It's a rarefied atmosphere. It gets to you. It gets to your brain and Bill enjoyed breathing it all in. Bill was always in the winning zone and it was inspirational as a player to hear him talk. He put fire in your belly and determination in your brain. That day in 1964 was a meeting with a man at the very peak of his career. Bill was hungry, ambitious; he had tasted success and liked the flavour. Bill might have done the Double, but his attitude was 'let's do the Treble'.

Not surprisingly, in Bill's world of management there was no place to find a seat and sit down and talk to him. He had found the formula for success and he guarded it jealously. Whatever Bill's secret was, he shared it with no one. Even at the training ground at Cheshunt, he still managed to keep his distance. He would never join the players for lunch. He would sit at a trellis table, sometimes with Eddie Baily and other times with coaches, but even when he was on his own, he never got up to go and sit with his players. Apart from football, he would never mix with the players. Eddie Baily told me he was just the same as a player in the push-and-run days. 'Bill,' he said, 'was never one of the boys.'

Although, as I say, he welcomed it when players married, he was not a big mixer with the players' wives either. In fact, he made it quite clear he wasn't happy to see women backstage in the football club. He would always be very polite and greet my wife, June, with a smile, but he was slightly embarrassed by it all. He was never relaxed or at ease at social meet-ups when women were around, especially within the confines of the Tottenham Hotspur Football Club.

In fact, one of my biggest bust-ups with Bill involved June. We were playing Arsenal a few miles up the road at Highbury in a League Cup semi-final in 1968 and there was a complete mix-up over the coaches that were taking the players' wives to the game. The club had hired lots of coaches on this occasion. One was to carry the Tottenham players and management, and the others were to take the players' wives and staff.

For some reason, and don't ask me how, June and Pat Jennings's wife, Eleanor, got on the wrong coach and had then been allowed to stay on it and travel with the Spurs players to the game. June felt very strongly that if she and Eleanor had been allowed to travel with their husbands, then all the other wives should have been allowed to do so as well.

Anyway, Bill got to hear June expressing her opinions in the boardroom after the game and he decided he had to make his position on match-day travelling clear, with no more misunderstandings. Bill insisted that all the players' wives had to travel in their own coach and furthermore added that any wives who travelled with their husbands were out of order. Bill left no room for doubt that, in his opinion, women had no place in football.

June, not surprisingly, was very upset about it all and was in tears. Naturally, I was far from happy. I could see June's reasoning and felt she had every right to make her point with Bill. I didn't like what Bill said, or the way he said it. We had one hell of a bust-up. I didn't agree with him, but I accepted it and that was exactly how it was with Bill. Unfortunately, it was an argument June was never going to win. When it came to a woman's place in football, Bill had very set views, and no matter what the situation, or who was involved, he was never going to change them. When Bill was manager at Tottenham, he had thoughts for one thing and one thing only, and that was football. Wives, I am afraid, were definitely way, way down in second place.

* * *

My co-author, Paul Trevillion, talked to the Preston wing-wizard Sir Tom Finney, who recalled his first encounter with Bill Nicholson, and Trevillion also reminds us that Bill Nicholson played a major role as a coach in the England set-up in Sweden during the 1958 World Cup. Don Howe was a member of that England side, and he lets us in on Bill Nicholson's tactical plan that put a stranglehold on the World Cup favourites, Brazil:

Sir Tom Finney on Bill Nicholson

'How far back does your memory go on Tottenham's Bill Nicholson?' I asked the pride of Preston, Sir Tom Finney.

'It stretches way back,' replied Finney. 'Right back to the 1940s when I was in the Army, stationed in Italy, and I played alongside Bill in two or three Army games. Looking back over all those years, I remember how struck I was by how fit he looked when I first met him. Bill was bursting with good health. There was no fitter man in the force, and he looked after his body. Bill didn't smoke, and just about everybody did in those days, and he might have had the occasional drink, but I never saw him with a glass in his hand. Bill was an Army PE instructor, so he worked out just about every day and it showed.

'In those Army football games I played with Bill, he stood out. Not because he did a lot on the ball – that wasn't Bill's style – but he had all the ability, was a good passer of the ball and could tackle. But above all, he was fit. He covered a lot of ground, did a tremendous amount of running and never took a breather. Didn't need to, he was that fit.

'Bill's level of fitness paid off. When he came out of the Army and played in the Tottenham push-and-run side, they passed the ball and ran into space and Bill was up to all that running. That side won the 1949–50 Second Division title and then the following year, 1951, they followed that up by winning the First Division championship, and Preston won the Second Division championship, so we both picked up medals.'

I then asked Finney if he remembered that 1951 was also the Festival of Britain year and that the Football Association celebrated by

Lilywhite magazine, 1952

inviting some of the top teams like France, Argentina and Portugal to play in the Festival internationals.

'I remember those games,' recalled Finney. 'Bill was picked to play against Portugal at Goodison Park. England won 5–2. Bill played well. We all played well and both Bill and I scored – Bill with his first kick of the ball. It was a bit special playing with Bill again, and like those games in the forces, he was full of running: the only difference being we didn't change back into our Army boots.'

I then asked Finney to tell me about the World Cup in Sweden in 1958 when they were both again on England duty.

'I was there as a player,' recalled Finney, 'and the England manager, Walter Winterbottom, had brought Bill along as a coach and trainer. I listened in on Bill's tactical planning on how England should play against the Brazilian team. I was injured, I wasn't in the side, but from the bench I saw Bill's words and tactical theories put into action, and they worked to perfection. The brilliant Brazilian side which went on to win the cup were held to a goal-less draw. I was very impressed and very proud of my old Army buddy.'

Finney continued, 'I played for Preston against Nicholson's Double side. We lost but I still enjoyed the games. In fact, I always enjoyed playing against Tottenham, way back to the days when Bill was a player and right throughout my career. Every season, I would search the fixture list to see when Preston were going to play Tottenham. I knew it would be a good afternoon. Both teams were good passing sides who played entertaining football in the right spirit of the game.'

Finney summed up: 'Looking back, they were all good memories with Bill, but still the most vivid is how fit he looked the first time I met him. Bill paid strict attention to his fitness all his life. Bill believed, and rightly so, that a footballer is an athlete and he can never perform to his maximum ability unless he is fully physically fit. When you get tired, your concentration suffers and that's when you make mistakes. Bill demanded absolute fitness of himself as a player and also of the players who played under him when he became a manager. Bill Nicholson may not have been the greatest player to pull on a football shirt, but of this I am sure – there has never been one fitter.'

Don Howe on Nicholson

'As a coach, Bill Nicholson was right up there with the very best,' Don Howe tells us. 'Take the 1958 World Cup in Sweden. I was in the England side that had qualified, scoring fifteen goals in their four matches, so we had a realistic chance of winning the trophy. But the Munich air disaster ripped the heart out of the team. The Manchester United trio, Roger Byrne, Duncan Edwards and Tommy Taylor, were now gone.

'In our second match in the tournament, we faced the favourites, Brazil, who had easily beaten Austria 3–0 in their first match. England had drawn with the Soviet Union 2–2 but what a price we paid. We lost arguably our best forward, Tom Finney, who got badly injured.

'The England manager, Walter Winterbottom, had brought along Bill Nicholson of Tottenham as a coach. He was Winterbottom's lieutenant, if you like. He watched the opposition and Winterbottom encouraged us to talk to him. Now, Winterbottom had tremendous faith and belief in Nicholson's coaching abilities so he allowed Nicholson, who had watched the Brazilians in their first match, to put his tactical ideas over and make the necessary defensive changes to stop the free-scoring Brazilians.

'I was England's right-back and Nicholson came over and said, "Don, have you ever played in a match where you have no left winger to mark?"

'I shook my head. "No, Bill."

'"You will tomorrow when you line up against Brazil," came back Nicholson.

'"Then, Bill," I replied, "I'm in for an easy afternoon."

'Nicholson took a step closer and, with a meaningful tone in his voice, said, "You're wrong, Don. It's not going to be an easy afternoon. You'll be doing *twice* the running: maybe even more. The Brazilian outside-left, Zagalo, plays as a withdrawn winger. He drops back to the halfway line. He operates from midfield, but don't you follow him. If you go looking for Zagalo, the space you leave behind they'll race into and Billy Wright will have to come out of the middle and cover. With you two now out of position, they'll be in."

'I listened as Nicholson drove his point home.

'"I want you to tuck in on Wright. Stay close to him. Never be more than ten yards away. Which means we now have you as an extra man in the midfield. There's no easy way through for the Brazilians: but don't take your eyes off Zagalo – he's the brains of their attack. Watch him, watch him, *watch him*, and if he should suddenly pop up on the left wing, make sure you are with him. It's going to take a tremendous amount of running and a tremendous amount of concentration, but you can do it, Don."

'Nicholson's plan worked to perfection. It was the first ever goal-less draw in the history of the World Cup finals and it proved to be the only game in which Brazil's goal machine failed to score on their way to winning the World Cup.

'In the dressing-room after the match, Nicholson was like a dog with two tails. He came over to me and said, "You did your job, Don."

'I said, "Thanks, Bill."

'Then Nicholson brought me down to earth. "But you gave the ball away four times!"

'I said, "Hold on, Bill. I must have made over forty passes and only missed with four."

'"I know, but four's four . . . try and cut it down."

'And Nicholson walked off.

'At the time, I thought what do you have to do to please the man? But when the day came and I was the England coach, I realised how right Nicholson was to say that. Good coaching is all about making a player better, and Nicholson was one of those coaches who always wanted you to raise the bar. He was always pushing you to up your level of performance, and if a coach doesn't do that, he's not doing his job. And believe me, Nicholson did one hell of a job on restricting Zagalo, emphasising he was the "brains" in the Brazilian attack. Zagalo was an ever-present in the sides that won the World Cup in 1958 and 1962.

'Not only that, Zagalo was the coach, the mastermind and the tactical genius behind the 1970 all-conquering Brazilian side which, even today, all the top coaches rate as the greatest free-flowing, attacking football team ever to win the famous World Cup trophy.

'I personally always got on very well with Nicholson and I put that down to the fact that I could pass the ball. I could tackle, head the ball and all that, but the strength of my game was my ability to pass a ball and Nicholson loved, really loved, good passers of a ball. That dated back to his playing days in the Tottenham push-and-run side. It was 'give and go', first-time, accurate passing with the players running off the ball into space.

'In my young days, I used to travel miles to watch that Tottenham team. I remember Nicholson. He was what you would call a 'tidy' passer of the ball. He was never over-ambitious and he never made a careless pass, so he hardly ever gave the ball away. But strangely enough, even though I was a defender like Nicholson, the one I went to watch, who could hurt a defence, I mean *really* hurt a defence with his passing, was the Tottenham inside-left and England international Eddie Baily. He was a fabulous player. He had plenty of flair, but what stood out was his exceptional first-time passing of the ball. It was absolutely breathtaking, and when you were on the end of a Baily pass, you didn't need to control the ball; Baily had done that job for you by putting just the right amount of weight on the ball, and you can't ask for more when receiving a pass from a teammate.

'Having said that, funnily enough, the thing I remember most about Baily is a goal he scored from 30 yards out! He spotted a small gap and the ball whistled in, never coming off the ground. That was a 30-yard pass at tracer-bullet speed. What a goal. I can still see it now and it's just as clear as the day Baily hammered it home.'

CHAPTER THREE

Bill and his Captains

Bill Nicholson had a very simple attitude towards just how far his Tottenham captains could go, and what they could do when it came to decision-making. It was this: when you are on the field, you are the manager.

Before the game, Bill would have his say and, like the rest of the Spurs players, I listened. It was the same at half-time and, of course, at the end of the game, but once the whistle went and the action started, it was down to me, his captain, to take charge and make decisions.

As his captain, I could, during a game, shuffle players around. I could get certain players to mark people. I could push an extra player forward if we needed a goal late in a game and I could, if the situation demanded it, bring up extra players for free-kicks and corner kicks.

This was what Bill wanted and, of course, it had worked beautifully for him over the years prior to me taking the helm in 1968. Take Danny Blanchflower, his Double-winning captain. Danny loved the responsibility Bill gave him as captain. As Danny was naturally a very domineering person, he was, in his mind, never wrong and he would argue constantly with Bill.

When Danny was forced to retire in 1964 and I arrived on the scene, it was Mackay who had taken over the responsibility of captain. Mackay was an entirely different character to Danny: he was a swashbuckling type, a fantastic leader, a marvellous captain. He was the dominant one in the Spurs squad and, as such, players followed him because of his inspirational leadership. Brian Clough recognised the leadership qualities in Dave. When Clough took Mackay to Derby County in 1968, they were in the bottom half of the Second Division. Clough immediately made him captain and Mackay led Derby back to the old First Division.

Where did I fit into this pattern? Well, I would like to think I offered Bill a little bit of both – Blanchflower and Mackay – and that is why it worked. Bill and I were a great team. As Blanchflower did, I would quite often question Bill's methods, especially his attacks on players after a game. Bill never held back, he would really have a go, and if I thought Bill was being unfair, I would step in. As for my predecessor, Dave Mackay, I offered the fighting qualities of the fiery Scotsman's leadership. I led by example, I led from the front. This was the sort of captain Bill wanted to follow Blanchflower and Mackay and he was happy that I combined qualities from both.

This was a great starting point, but Bill would want more. He would insist his captains earned the respect of each and every player in the squad. They had to earn the captain's badge. I had to earn mine, and Martin Peters, when he took over from me, had to earn his, even though he was a World Cup winner! After Peters, it was Steve Perryman, and it was no different: he had to win his 'spurs', as it were, in front of the other players. Perryman did earn their respect and he went on to captain the side in a similar way to myself, with the defiant attitude of 'never say die'.

There is no doubt that Bill knew the sort of strong character he wanted as a captain and he would find that player who had the ability to adopt the role of manager on the pitch. That's one of the most vital jobs of good football management.

I quickly learned from Bill what made a good captain and what qualities to look for in a player. I can remember that, when I landed my first job in management at Brighton, I turned up on the first day of training and, without knowing anything about the Brighton squad, I pointed to one player and said to the coach, 'He's the captain of the team, isn't he?'

My coach, Ken Gutteridge, said to me, 'Yes, you are right. That's Brian Horton.'

I could see immediately he was a leader and he did it extremely well. Horton became my manager on the pitch, and he was a very successful one. Horton was a midfield player and, for me, that is where a captain should play. I have always believed that for a goalkeeper or striker to captain a side is wrong, because often that type of player is miles away from the action at crucial times in the game.

Nicholson, too, thought like this. If you look at his captains over the years, they were all midfield players. Blanchflower (midfield), Mackay (midfield), myself (midfield), Peters (midfield) and Perryman (midfield). All Bill's captains played in midfield – a role which allowed them to operate at the heart of the action most of the time.

Another manager who thought like Nicholson when it came to captains was Sir Alf Ramsey, when he was England boss. Sir Alf looked for leaders as captains and again, preferred a midfield player in the captain's role, with Bobby Moore a classic example. When Moore was injured in Malta for an important European Championship qualifier, I couldn't believe it when he chose yours truly to captain the side. I'm sure the fact that I was a midfield player helped Sir Alf with his final choice.

My policy as the Spurs captain with a player who wasn't carrying out Bill's instructions would be to have a few firm words and do my best to put that player right. On the other hand, if I found a player who was having a poor game, I would in no way hammer him. Supporters might think that's the thing to do, so they voice their feelings and have a go, but that's not right. No player goes out to play poorly. Every player who goes out on that pitch goes out to perform to their very best, but being human, as we are, it doesn't always happen like that. One week, 75 per cent of a player's game will be good, with 25 per cent poor, and the next week it's possible for it to be the complete opposite. I always reckoned that if a team has seven to eight players on form, playing better than the seven to eight players in the opposing team, then you will win the game. Twenty-two players run out onto that pitch and all twenty-two want to play well. But nature dictates that they can't, so if a player is making mistake after mistake, I would go up to him and say, 'Hey, don't try and play the difficult balls, play the safe, easy pass until you get your confidence back.' On the other hand, if a teammate wasn't playing to orders and marking an opponent properly, I would literally go up to him, grab him, pull him into his correct position and say, 'LOOK, here's the man you are marking, pick him up, get tighter, don't let him spin to the left, push him onto his bad foot.'

That was the way I tackled it. And this was basically what Nicholson would have done in the dressing-room. The only difference was that it was me, his captain, doing it for him on the pitch until Bill could have his say at half-time.

What I always tried to do was to take the match 'blueprint' Nicholson and I had worked on all week as we prepared for the game onto the pitch. But players are not machines, they are human beings – they can't be pre-programmed – so it didn't always work out as we had planned. Then I would change things, tell players what to do differently, because that was my job as captain, to make decisions during the game. That was what Nicholson expected of me. If a player didn't like what I said, or what I ordered him to do, then he was free to have a go at me at half-time or after the game.

I am often asked just how far would Nicholson allow me to change his orders once a game was under way. I might have been Bill's appointed manager on the pitch, but were there any limits I had to adhere to? Yes, there were limits, as I found out one day at Old Trafford when we were playing Manchester United. Believing that I was in my rights, I made a substitution during the match. After the game, when Bill and I were together on our own, I got the biggest ten-minute rollicking I had ever had off Bill. He stormed at me and shouted, 'Don't you ever make decisions like that again. I make those decisions about who comes off and who goes on.' That happened very early on in my reign as captain and I never did that again. I found out, in no uncertain terms, the limits of my responsibilities.

One area where Bill and I had different opinions was referees. Bill didn't like his players or captain to question the referee's decision. Bill's attitude was always the same – you are never going to change the referee's mind. I must admit now that I didn't take much notice of Bill's stance. I would challenge referees' decisions if I felt they had made a mistake and I still think the same way today. Refs are there to make decisions and if they get them wrong, then players are fully entitled to complain about it.

Yes, I agree, every referee goes out to do his best on the pitch, but sometimes they will get it wrong, which is only natural, but if they get it wrong then they should get a right earful – even more so in the modern game, where so much can ride on one vital decision by the referee. A referee has to take some stick, and if he doesn't like it then the answer is don't be in the business of football refereeing.

But Nicholson saw it all differently. I can still see him sitting in the dressing-room before a game telling us, 'Look, lads, you're not going to change the referee's mind, so it's a total waste of time arguing.'

As I've explained, I just couldn't take that on board when I was out on the pitch, captaining the side. So I would, if I felt the referee was wrong, question and even argue with him and there were times when I really did have a go, but looking back I now have to admit that wise old Bill was right, because we never got one – not one – decision changed. Mind you, it was a referee who gave me the biggest laugh I ever had as Tottenham captain.

We were playing Manchester United at Old Trafford in a night game in front of 60,000 people and I went up to the centre circle for the kick-off and to shake hands with the United skipper, Denis Law, and to hopefully win the toss of the coin, which I always considered very important. I saw the referee looking a little agitated and a little flustered as he was frantically searching his pockets, digging deep, searching for something. Then I twigged it. He couldn't find the coin to toss up with!

You can imagine it. A packed house at Old Trafford in full voice. The two teams warming up and there in the centre circle, confusion reigned as the three of us looked at each other as if to say 'What do we do now?'

The referee made a quick decision. He said to both of us, 'Look, what we'll do is make out we're going to spin the coin up in the air.'

Denis, quick as a flash, chipped in and said, 'Heads!'

So we were playing our own little game in the centre circle, because we never had a coin. It all looked in order from the terraces, but Denis, myself and the ref were making it up as we went along.

Anyway, when the 'invisible' coin did come down, Denis shouted, 'THERE YOU ARE, IT'S HEADS!'

I yelled back, 'NO IT'S NOT, IT'S TAILS!'

Then Denis and I started a big argument over a coin that never existed. We even made it look real by bending down and pretending to pick up a coin to give back to the ref, who by this time had lost control and he knew he had to make a swift decision before it got completely out of hand.

He drew the whole bizarre episode to an end when he turned to me and said, 'Look, Alan, because you are the away team you can kick off.'

Both Denis and I laughed and then we got on with it. It was Spurs to kick off.

I don't think I ever told Bill about that centre-circle comedy, but despite his image of being a dour Yorkshireman, Nicholson did enjoy a good laugh and I am sure that Manchester fiasco would have brought a rare Nicholson laugh and left him with a wide smile on his face. It certainly did mine.

Another game which I remember for the referee's role was no laughing matter. It certainly didn't bring a smile to my face. This time, it took place at Manchester City's old Maine Road ground. It was December 1967 and Bill and the Spurs team arrived at the City ground to find it completely covered in snow and ice. Bill and captain Dave Mackay went to see the referee, as they were both convinced the pitch was not only unplayable, it was highly dangerous. In those days, there was no under-soil heating or anything like that. Bill and Mackay were of the same mind – the game should not be started – but the referee, possibly taking into account the huge crowd, decided to go ahead and see how things went.

Spurs had no option but to play, but we soon found we were slipping and sliding all over the field. Even so, we took the lead, but it was clear that the City boys were somehow managing to keep on their feet and they were literally skating rings round us. It emerged later that they had played a clever trick with their footwear. Aware that the pitch was not far short of an ice rink, they changed their studs just prior to the kick-off. They replaced their normal studs with the old leather ones and removed a small piece of leather off the top of each of them. They then filed down the exposed nails to make them safe, while allowing them to show through just enough to get a grip on the icy pitch.

With such an advantage, it was only a matter of time before City took control and, sure enough, Colin Bell soon equalised. From then on, they ran us ragged and further goals from Mike Summerbee, Neil Young and Tony Coleman saw City run out easy winners 4–1.

The match is now part of City folklore and is still keenly remembered in the pubs and clubs of Manchester. It even made the front cover of the Manchester City Football Club's Christmas card, which showed a picture of the Colin Bell goal with the rather clever title, 'Ballet on Ice'.

Those two points that City took that day proved more than useful. They went on to win the title with 58 points, with Manchester United in second place with 56 points. At the time, Nicholson and the Spurs players were furious. Throughout the game, we were begging the ref to call a halt and at half-time Nicholson went to see him and strongly expressed his view that the pitch was not fit for football, but the ref wouldn't have it. 'We play on,' he told Nicholson.

After the game, Bill and the Spurs boys were totally unaware of what had gone on in the City dressing-room before the match. Bill was no more disappointed than he normally was after a defeat, but if he had known the full story he would have gone ballistic. Of that I am sure.

However, I still feel the referee made two major blunders that day. Firstly, he should never have started the game, and secondly he should have checked both teams' footwear a bit more closely.

It was a disappointed group of players who gathered the following week at our Cheshunt training ground to sort out what had gone wrong, but Bill knew he couldn't go through his normal post-match routine of working on things which hadn't happened as planned. On this occasion, he knew it was a 'one-off' in conditions not meant for football.

During my reign as captain, Bill would normally call me over for a cup of tea and we would analyse the previous game, carefully paying attention to areas which hadn't worked as we had planned in our blueprint for the game. We worked together on that blueprint all week before a match, but often once the game began the plan had to be abandoned because the opposing team had arrived on the scene with their own script.

Nicholson, with his photographic mind, was brilliant at pinpointing just what happened in a match, and it was a lesson in itself to sit with him on the day after a match that I had captained and get his views from the bench.

Although, as the captain, I had a close relationship with Bill, it was never unhealthily close. Decisions like team selection and dropping of players who weren't on form were all done by Bill and rightly so. He knew exactly what he was doing, and he was seldom wrong.

I never believed a captain should get too close to a manager. On the pitch, yes, Bill liked me to be his right arm – and more – but off it, he was the boss. Some managers and captains get much too close. They are constantly on the phone to each other and you do wonder who is really calling the shots: the captain or the manager? With Nicholson, there was never any doubt: he was the boss. He knew exactly what he needed to know about each and every one of his players; he didn't need to ask me, and, all the time I was his captain, he never did.

As for personal problems off the park involving players, again Bill would never involve me. Indeed, the only major personal problem I was ever aware of involved me directly, along with my wife, June. We had a very nasty car accident – June had been catapulted straight through the windscreen and was, at one time, close to death. We both ended up in hospital and, within 24 hours, Nicholson had been to visit me. I was in a very poor way, with cracked ribs, etc. After a week, I was allowed home, but June was to have a much longer stay in hospital.

Anyway, I was resting a badly aching body at home when the doorbell rang. I was hobbling about in my pyjamas and dressing gown and I wondered who it could be. Yes, you've guessed it, it was Bill.

'Come in, Bill, take a seat,' I told him and hobbled off to make him a cup of tea.

There I was, all strapped up, aching all over, wondering why Bill hadn't asked me to sit down and offered to make the tea, when he came over, looked me straight in the face and said, 'Alan, you're looking fantastic!'

I thought, 'Funny', as the late, great comedian Dudley Moore used to say.

Then Bill hit me with the big one. 'Alan,' he said, 'I want you to play against Manchester United on Saturday.'

I said, 'Bill, you've got to be raving mad. How can I play? I've got cracked ribs.'

Bill went on: 'No, I'm not mad – we've got quite a few injuries and I need your inspiration on the field, if not physically, *verbally*.'

I said again, 'Bill, you've got to be joking.' But he wasn't!

He said, 'Alan, you'll be fine. What we'll do is let you rest up until the end of the week, get you a car to bring you over to Cheshunt and get you out on the training pitch.'

'Bill, I can't believe what you're saying,' I said, still shocked, but I was quickly realising Nicholson meant every word.

In those days, you never argued with a manager. Today, a player would just say 'no way'. So I had to go along with it and I was taken over to the Cheshunt training ground by car.

I hobbled out onto the field with our trainer, Cecil Poynton, and I somehow managed to do a lap of the pitch, which was farcical and a total waste of time in my physical state.

Poynton ran over to me and, to my amazement, said, 'You're in great shape, fantastic: you'll do for me. You'll play against Manchester United on Saturday.'

That was it. I was in the team to play Manchester United. During the game, I played the ball eight to ten times, no more, but I was very loud with the verbals. We were losing 1–0 with fifteen minutes to go, when Jimmy Greaves turned on the magic, scored two great goals and we won 2–1.

It was a struggle, but I managed to literally crawl off the pitch straight into a waiting car, which took me home, and I collapsed into bed and remembered nothing else.

When Bill told you to do something, you had to do it. It was as simple as that. Nicholson had his win over United and his big gamble had paid off. It was a ruthless time for footballers. You had to obey your manager. Today, a player wouldn't be allowed near a football pitch after a car crash. But back in the late '60s, we all put our bodies, when injured, through agonies, and it's one of the biggest reasons why today so many players of that generation have ended up having to have surgery on their backs, knees and hips etc. I was captain of Tottenham Hotspur, Bill Nicholson was my manager and I felt it was my duty to put my body through the pain barrier. They were tough times. It was a very hard, even brutal culture. That was football in the '60s.

For instance, if two players had a personality clash at Tottenham, Nicholson had his way of sorting it out. He wouldn't call in a counsellor like they do today. He wouldn't ask me for an opinion. Nicholson was always happy to see it sorted out with a bare-knuckle fist fight during a five-a-side game in the gym! That was the no-nonsense culture which was the norm at Spurs. Cecil Poynton, who was our trainer and man with the 'magic sponge', used to love watching footballers coming to blows, swinging away, fighting each other. Nicholson would watch the action and then, at the first sight of blood, he would jump in and split the two fighting men. What it showed was a man's desire to win. It was a brutal solution, but that's how arguments between players were settled.

Today, a player would probably sue a teammate if he even touched him in an argument. In those days, down at Tottenham, you would go home with a cut eye, split lip or a bloody nose. But on the following morning, it would all be forgotten and you would be laughing and training as mates. And I tell you this, when it came to Saturday and match day, all grievances were forgotten. You were all mates: you went out there and you fought for them and they fought for you, and that's how matches were won.

A question I am often asked is what was the one overriding trait that Bill Nicholson had that made him such a winner. I always give the same answer: he was meticulous. Every detail, no matter how small, how minute, in a build-up to a match, Nicholson had it covered.

I once asked the former Arsenal goalkeeper Bob Wilson what he believed was Arsène Wenger's secret.

'Alan,' said Bob, 'Arsène is meticulous in all his planning at Arsenal.'

Funny that, both Nicholson and Wenger have the same secret to their success – and they both led their teams to the Double.

* * *

When my co-author, Paul Trevillion, spoke to former England captain Joe Mercer, he found Joe full of admiration for Bill Nicholson as a player and also as a manager who excelled in the transfer market . . .

Joe Mercer on Bill Nicholson

I was talking to Joe Mercer, who in his playing days captained England, Everton and Arsenal. We were discussing an article published in the

Sunday Times in which the highly respected football journalist Brian Glanville and I had assessed the merits of the England captain, Bobby Moore. Acting as referee in the article was Joe Mercer, who rated Moore a better skipper than he was a player. I switched the conversation to Bill Nicholson by asking if Tottenham, by not making Bill Nicholson captain (although he stood in on the odd occasion), had missed out. Mercer, as always, had an answer and it dated back to 1937!

'I was playing for Everton in a Cup tie at White Hart Lane; we were leading Tottenham 3–1 with five minutes to go,' said Mercer. 'I centred the ball and Arthur Rowe, who was then the Spurs centre-half, mistimed his tackle on our centre-forward, Dixie Dean. It was a penalty. But the Spurs players persuaded the ref to consult the linesman. He ruled the ball had gone out of play before I centred it and, if I am honest, it had – only just, but it had – so it was a throw-in to Spurs. The Everton players were still arguing when Spurs went straight down and scored. They scored again and then again – three goals in four minutes – and Everton were out of the Cup.

'A couple of years later, I was with Arthur Rowe and we talked about that match and the name Bill Nicholson cropped up. Rowe told me Nicholson was one for the future. He had just made his first-team debut and Rowe, a good judge of a player, believed Nicholson had not only the ability but the mental strength and determination to go all the way.

'"He's not one of those defenders who gets caught in two minds," said Rowe. "He's quick to weigh up all the possibilities and doesn't commit himself until he's sure he can get the ball. Then he goes in and wins it, and he doesn't give it away, he knocks it off to a teammate."'

Mercer paused for a second then repeated Rowe's words: '"Nicholson weighed up all the possibilities and didn't commit himself until he was sure he could get the ball." I believe Rowe, with those few words, just about summed up Nicholson's game. He never gambled. He was never tempted into playing a ball that would get you out of your seats if there was an element of risk. He was a safe, reliable defender whose best work went unnoticed because he played his football without frills. Nicholson was the type of player you checked for on the programme to see if he was playing.'

Mercer went on: 'You had to play with him or against him to

appreciate what a great defender he was, and when the opposing manager was looking for a weakness in the Tottenham defence, the name Nicholson never came up.

'In the Spurs Arthur Rowe push-and-run defence, Nicholson at right-half was the anchor, but there were no chains on the captain Ronnie Burgess at left-half – he was a magnificent player who stole the show in every match he played. Burgess was a born leader. He had only to step onto the pitch to stamp his personality on the game and his tremendous drive and non-stop running made him an inspirational skipper who was always ready to take a risk, go forward and have a shot at goal.

'Spurs manager Arthur Rowe had the best of both worlds. In Burgess, he had a dynamic captain who led from the front and in Nicholson he had a disciplined defender who set a captain's example. Nicholson was the one in defence who kept order and maintained its shape, even more so than the right-back, Alf Ramsey.

'I believe,' emphasised Mercer, 'Nicholson was happy Burgess was made captain. Bill was never one to search out the spotlight. I am sure if he had been Spurs captain and led the team to glory, he would have stepped aside unnoticed and left it to someone else to lift up the Cup.

'Throughout his career, Nicholson has stayed in the background – never gambled or made a hasty decision: that's why he's never had to change one. This, of course, is his biggest strength as Tottenham's manager in the transfer market. When he makes up his mind, Nicholson moves with the same conviction he showed as a player. Unnoticed, with an unshakeable belief, he gets his man and another player is on Spurs' books – and I know this to my cost.'

Mercer shook his head and went on: 'When I was manager at Sheffield United, I went to see a young lad playing for Alloa in the Scottish Second Division. The boy had good balance, a great first touch, moved well, found space and knew where the goal was. He had it all, but he was very frail. Even so, I thought I'll go for him. But my chief scout, who was with me, was adamant the lad wasn't strong enough. Like a fool, I listened and I passed, but I should have backed my own judgement.

'Nicholson did back his judgement. He'd done his homework, discovered the lad was a champion cross-country runner, then he went in unnoticed, paid £20,000 and John White was a Tottenham player. The day I saw White, I could have signed him for as little as £3,500.

'I phoned Nicholson,' went on Mercer, 'and told him, "With White, you'll win the title." And Tottenham should have done, but they slipped up at the finish.'

With that, Mercer was off.

The reason White did not prove Mercer right and Tottenham didn't go on to win the First Division title was down to another young man, who played for the newly promoted Fulham. At the start of that 1959–60 season, the top First Division managers looked down their fixture list, saw the name Fulham and marked them down for four points, as home and away wins. In those days, it was two points for a win and one for a draw. But Fulham were to prove no pushovers. Tottenham, the title favourites, with their team full of internationals had to settle for a draw both times they met and those two dropped points cost them the title. Burnley were champions, with 55 points compared to Wolves' 54 and Tottenham's 53, although Spurs had a vastly superior goal average to both teams.

* * *

How did Fulham manage to rob Tottenham of those two vital championship points? Alan Mullery, who played in the Fulham side, takes up the story:

The Fulham team had bags of experience. A lot of the players had represented their country and in Johnny Haynes we had the England captain. In goal, the spectacular Tony Macedo was unbeatable on his day. Young George Cohen, strong in the tackle, lightning fast, was always prepared to go forward. Jimmy Langley had a left foot that was capable of picking locks. Jimmy Hill could run all day and Graham Leggat was always good for a goal. In fact, every one in the Fulham team could play a bit.

We were not afraid of Tottenham and we gave them problems. We knew Nicholson would not restrict Blanchflower or Mackay to close-mark Haynes. Those two players loved to go forward, leaving the nearest man to pick up Haynes, which never worked, so Haynes with

Tottenham Weekly Herald, 1959–60 season

his inch-perfect passing repeatedly had Tottenham on the back foot. I had the job of close-marking 'the ghost', John White.

Our manager, Bedford Jezzard, instructed me to get inside White's shirt and I did just that. Every move White made on the field, I was with him. Every blade of grass White covered, so did I. White, a cross-country champion, was never still; he was constantly on the move, searching and trying to make space. But I was fit – I could run too – and I was with him. Every time a Tottenham player looked to pass to White, they saw double. I was with him. The truth is, I stuck so close to White, I could actually hear his heart beating!

Both times we played Tottenham, it was my job to close-mark White and he failed to show. Both games ended 1–1 and those two dropped points cost Tottenham the title.

* * *

Joe Mercer was right on two counts: Tottenham should have won the title that season and Nicholson always did his homework. Alan Mullery's name was now firmly fixed in Nicholson's memory bank, as Nicholson admitted later.

'In those two games we played against Fulham,' said Nicholson, 'I knew when I needed a replacement for Blanchflower, I had only to make the short trip to Fulham. Alan Mullery fitted the role perfectly.'

CHAPTER FOUR

Nicholson–Baily: How it Worked

Probably no one featured more in Bill Nicholson's amazing life than Eddie Baily. They were teammates in the all-conquering Spurs side of the '50s, which won the Second Division and First Division titles in successive seasons. They then joined forces again at White Hart Lane in the early '60s, this time with Eddie Baily as Bill Nicholson's assistant-manager and coach.

As a coach, Baily was regarded as something of a hard man who favoured players who would run and run all day. But in the Tottenham push-and-run side, he was a skilful ball player with a lot of flair. He won eleven England call-ups, which was ten more than his boss, Bill. Indeed, it's impossible to write a book on Nicholson without giving Baily at least a chapter. Eddie was brought on board by Bill shortly before I joined the club in 1964, and the part he played in Spurs' continued success after its Double team had begun to be disbanded just cannot be overestimated. Sad to say, though, the importance of Eddie's influence has too often been ignored and Eddie, rightly so in my opinion, is not best pleased about it.

Here is a man who was with Bill every step of the way, and yet is the forgotten man in the Spurs success story of the late '60s and early '70s. I needed to set the record straight and was honoured when Eddie, now 80, granted me an interview in early 2005. We settled down at

Eddie's Hertfordshire home one sunny morning and talked about the good old days. It was a memorable meeting, especially as Eddie will always have a place in my heart as it was Eddie who accompanied Bill in all the talks prior to my signing for Tottenham.

What quickly emerged was the depth of Eddie's disillusionment with the way he was treated by not only the club but also by Bill, who was never one to say too much to the media and so he never gave Eddie the public acknowledgement he felt he deserved. Eddie was also disappointed with Bill because he did not put his name forward as the next manager when Nicholson resigned in 1974.

As I sat there listening to this marvellous cockney character unburdening himself of years of pent-up hurt, I have to admit I felt for him. He should have had more accolades. In the very successful trophy-winning Clough-and-Taylor partnership, just look at the recognition which went to Taylor. Make no mistake, Nicholson and Baily were on the same level. I was there to see it. I saw them work together as a team, and now I have to admit I never once saw any tell-tale signs of disharmony between them. So Eddie's real feelings, which were now being expressed to me, all came as quite a shock.

I am fully aware that for Taylor to get so much recognition as a number two was unusual, and that not many assistant-managers get this much credit or even deserve it, but Eddie was one who I believe did get something of a very raw deal.

From the players' point of view, Eddie was one of the lads. We trusted him and he was the man who took a lot off Bill's back. We knew he would never run to Bill with any stories and a close bond was in place between us. He was a fun character and enjoyed a laugh, which all went to building a tremendous team spirit at Tottenham.

I soon had Eddie in stitches when I reminded him of the times Jimmy Greaves would nick Eddie's bicycle on some of the long-distance runs and would arrive back at the training ground after having only done half-a-mile of running, while poor Eddie had to run back with the players after discovering his cycle had gone. In those days, Eddie would enjoy the joke and wouldn't dream of going to Bill and reporting the incident. He would accept that that was the fun thing that went on with certain characters. Indeed, Eddie was one of the characters in the Spurs set-up – a typical cockney character.

I had always known him as just that, even before I became a Spurs player. In fact, Eddie and I go back a long way, all the way to my first game for Fulham in the '50s. I was just 17 and Eddie was captain of the opposition, Leyton Orient. Before the kick-off, Eddie shook hands with our captain, Johnny Haynes, and the referee spun the coin. I was standing just behind the two skippers during the warm-up and I heard Eddie say to the referee, 'Ref, I want to ask you a question.'

'What's that, Eddie?' enquired the ref.

'Is there any swearing today?'

The ref came back like a shot: 'Eddie, there is no swearing at all.'

So Eddie carried it on: 'What about swearing at your own players?'

By this time, the ref had lost his patience and he said, 'I've told you, Eddie: no swearing at all.'

At that, Eddie blasted out, 'F***ing 'ell.'

That was Eddie – a true character both as a player and coach, and although Bill was the figurehead and deservedly took many of the plaudits at Spurs during the Nicholson–Baily years, the role of Eddie Baily should never be underestimated.

This role had its beginning when Eddie was coaching at Leyton Orient. Eddie remembered the incident clearly: 'I was coaching at the Orient in the 1962–63 season and one day who should pop down to Brisbane Road to watch a game but Bill Nicholson. I hadn't spoken to Bill for years as, after I left Spurs as a player, Bill stayed on as part of the coaching staff. After the match, Bill waited for me and asked me, "How's it going?"

'I was shocked to see him and wondered what on earth he was doing coming to the Orient. I joked to Bill, "You haven't come to see a good team, have you?"

'Bill laughed and said, "No. I've come because I want to talk to you. I've lost my assistant-manager. We have a good team at Spurs and I need someone who can come to White Hart Lane and help me with the coaching and training."

'Bill went on: "I remember you were one of those types who wasn't frightened what you said or who you said it to. I need someone like you who can get at players if it's needed."

'I was getting the message. Bill wanted me to get under the skin of someone who he didn't want to be nasty to, but once I had started to rattle the player Bill would then step in to make his point. Yes, I got the picture.

'Bill was clearly impressed with the coaching job I had done at Orient – we even had a spell in the old First Division, which was equivalent to today's Premiership. I was always confident of my ability and I emphasised that point to Bill. "I think I am as good a coach as you, Bill," I told him.

'It sounded good, but the one thing Bill hadn't mentioned was money. I was on a player's contract at the Orient and was earning £20 a week. "I think, Bill, you should double my wages," I told him.

'Bill told me he would talk to the directors, so I said to him, "Surely you now tell the directors what to do. You are the top boss in English football – you've just won the Double. And what about a contract? You know I've never liked the way they do certain things at Spurs. I do need to know who I will be working for. Will it be you or the club?"

'I asked Bill, "Do *you* have a contract with the club?"

'And, to my surprise, he said, "No, I haven't got a contract."

'I can't imagine that happening today. After all, Bill had just made Spurs the biggest club in the land.

'Eventually, everything was sorted out and I was delighted to join up with Bill again. I worked with Bill from 1962–1974 and, during most of the time that we worked together, he was very good to me and looked after me well. But towards the end, Bill and I began to fall out. In 1974, when it all ended, I have to admit I was very disappointed at the way Bill and the club behaved, but now that I know all the facts I can see that Bill himself was under a lot of unfair pressure and his treatment of me is now more understandable.

'When Bill was looking around for his successor, he began to be very secretive. I knew full well he had Danny Blanchflower, Johnny Giles and Gordon Jago up in his office on their own. But he would never tell me that he was going to interview these guys for the job. So I grabbed the bull by the horns one day and said to Bill, "Hey, what about me? Why don't they stick me in the job? I know all the players. I can handle them."

'Bill's reply was short and sweet: "Eddie, I don't think the directors would have you. You've been on overseas tours with the likes of chairman Sidney Wale and you've had rows and fallen out with them."'

Eddie admits now that indeed he did have various fall-outs with the directors on overseas tours but still feels that after all his years at the club and his special relationship with the players, Bill should have at the very least put his name forward and given him a strong endorsement. It clearly still grates with Eddie, who still has a theory that Bill wanted Blanchflower to get the job because he had come to an agreement with Danny that if he got the manager's job then he would move upstairs and oversee it all. It is certainly sad that such a successful partnership should end with a certain amount of acrimony on one side and I have to admit I was surprised by the strength of Eddie's feelings.

He went on: 'I have to say, I was hurt by it all. Bill was a great coach, a family man, an honest man, but where I wasn't sure about him was when it came to sticking up for his staff.

'I've always believed that you cannot run a business, however good you are, without having a staff member you can rely on. I believe he relied on me on lots of occasions, from coaching to joining him on scouting missions prior to signing a new player, etc.

'Yes, sure, Bill was a good coach but when I joined the club I had a lot to bring to the table. Bill, I'm sure, had checked me out carefully. He threw me in at the deep end. As a coach, Bill was meticulous, but when I joined the club, he had to start listening to me and he hadn't listened to too many people as he had run the show on his own. So in those early days, we had one or two heated debates about coaching. In the end, it worked very well, but in my own mind I made a big contribution to the continued success of Spurs.

'After all, I had handled a Tottenham first team full of superstars. Not everyone could do that. Top players are cocky and you've got to match 'em. I could match 'em. They couldn't beat me. When it came to appointing a new boss, things like that should count. Bill knew I could handle the biggest stars in the game.

'As you know, Alan, another role Bill was happy for me to fulfil was that of socialiser with the players. Part of my job was to mix with the boys. I would go out with you all for a drink after a game and Bill never, ever, did that. He was never a socialiser. He always gave you the impression that he didn't want to mix with his players. He never mixed in the Spurs team in the '50s as a player. He was never one of the boys, but in his defence he never put a foot wrong. He was always smart, always meticulous, always training and a credit to Tottenham.

'He was your typical dour Yorkshireman and I was the cocky cockney. Put the two together and we had a winning management partnership. But Bill needed me as the second part of the jigsaw.

'Bill, I must say, had his share of good luck, which every great manager needs. Take the case of Dave Mackay, the driving force in the 1961 Double side. Bill would say that Dave was his best-ever buy, but Lady Luck played a large role in Dave's signing. At the time, Bill was after Mel Charles of Swansea, but Mel got injured and so Bill switched his attention to Mackay because he had been tipped off by a scout in Scotland that Dave was an excellent player. So Bill took Mackay, but it could so easily have been Mel Charles. Such was Mackay's influence on that Double side, the entire Bill Nicholson story could have been a different one if Mel hadn't had that injury. That's how life goes.

'I don't want to come over as a bitter old man. I'm not. In the main, I haven't a bad word to say about Bill. What we did together both as players in the '50s and later as a coaching duo I will always be very proud of and the odd problem at the end won't cloud a great memory.'

Despite Eddie's careful and understandable desire not to spoil the memories of a legendary partnership, I was anxious to probe a little deeper and asked Eddie just why he thought Bill was a little aloof from his staff.

Eddie had his theories: 'I just had a feeling that the root cause of this was that he felt he was on a planet of his own because he had done the Double in 1961. In those days, you must remember that the Double of FA Cup and league championship really was the Holy Grail. Bill really was worshipped not only by Spurs fans but by English, indeed, British, football as a whole.

'My gut feeling, as I say, is that until Bertie Mee came along and did the Double at Arsenal in 1971, he did feel almost untouchable. He did like the fact that until Mee came along he was the first manager to win the Double since the boss of Aston Villa in 1897. Indeed, only Villa in 1897 and Preston in 1889 had done the Double prior to Bill's 1961 achievement. So it was a truly massive feather in Bill's cap.

'I always felt Bill liked the tag of the first manager to do the Double since 1897, and who can blame him? In an ideal world, he would have loved to have kept that solo 'Double King' tag, but, as you know, in life nothing is forever.'

When the curtain finally did come down on the Nicholson–Baily reign in 1974, I had already left the club to return to Fulham, so I was intrigued to hear Eddie's version of the final days of the empire.

'Bill was really down towards the end,' said Eddie, 'and, looking back, I have a feeling he had got a sniff of some unrest in the boardroom. I feel that Sidney Wale wanted to be the boss – after all, he was chairman – but such was Bill's standing it appeared to almost everyone that Bill Nicholson *was* Tottenham. He wasn't. It was Sidney Wale.

'I mean, I had a big bust-up with Bill over the fact that suddenly this journalist, Hunter Davies, was coming everywhere with us. I mean everywhere – including the dressing-room. That was a sign to me that Bill was losing his overall authority. I said to Bill, "What's going on here?"

'Bill said, "Well, *someone* has given Hunter permission to follow us for a year and write about it in a book."

'So I said, "Well, *who* has?"

'All Bill could say was, "I don't know."

'I was surprised by Bill's answer. My guess is that it was the chairman – but who knows? I wasn't happy, especially as Hunter was none too complimentary about me! As it turned out, the book, *The Glory Game* (Mainstream, 1972), went on to become one of football's all-time classics, but at the time it was a sign of Bill's weakening power at the club.'

Eddie, as he says, was upset when the book was first published in 1972 and I am equally sure some of the players were surprised to read Hunter's warts-and-all account of a season with Spurs. What I am also sure about is that never again will a club give access to a journalist to go literally everywhere with a team for an entire season. Hunter certainly got himself a scoop.

My co-author, Paul Trevillion, also features in the book, as it was written during his groundbreaking promotional work at Don Revie's Leeds United – but it was Eddie who took some hard knocks, due to his aggressive language as a coach. It was common knowledge that Eddie was none too pleased with the book at the time.

And neither it seems was Bill himself, who admits as much in his own book, *Glory Glory: My Life with Spurs* (Macmillan, 1984). Bill goes on to say that he was upset that Hunter had got access and that, with hindsight, he would not have let it happen. But, as Eddie says, did he have the final decision? It seems not.

In 2001, Mainstream published a new edition of this book and interestingly Hunter wrote in his introduction, 'If I did upset [Eddie], then I do regret it.' He went on, 'In the book, Eddie does shout and swear quite a bit, but then he's a coach. That's what coaches do. And in far stronger terms than anything I reported. I like to think it did give a glimpse of the real world of football.'

As Eddie says, looking back, this whole episode was a symptom of Bill's loss of overall power at the Club and was a classic sign that the curtain was about to come down. When it did, it was traumatic.

Eddie remembers: 'Instead of getting better, things got a lot worse. Bill believed he was going to appoint the next manager but it never happened. As we all know now, it was Terry Neill who got 'the hot seat. Nobody, apart from Terry Neill and the chairman, will ever know what really went on. I always felt that the chairman let Bill go down his own route for finding his successor, but he was always going to make the big decision. Terry Neill was his choice. A strange one, to say the least.

'The big day came and Terry Neill arrived at Tottenham. I can remember him marching into my office and saying, "Hello, Eddie. How are you?"

'"Not very happy," I said. "What's happening to me?"

'"Well, I'll be bringing Wilf Dixon with me," said Terry.

'At that, I said, "Well, I'll clear my desk and go."

'"Oh, don't worry. Bill is going to sort you out," was Terry's response.

'Anyway, Bill and I had to go up to the official press meeting to unveil Terry Neill as the new Tottenham manager and it was all very embarrassing. Bill and I stood right at the back looking very sheepish and feeling very uncomfortable. This was not the way the two of us should have been treated; we deserved a lot better. I had had enough. I told Bill, "I'm going home. If you want me, I'm there."

'I had to wait until the club gave me three months' salary, and I then went and signed on at Walthamstow Labour Exchange. So much for the glamour of football.'

Despite the painful end of the Nicholson–Baily partnership and the underlying resentment which seems to have been bubbling away on Eddie's side, it would be totally wrong to end this chapter on a negative note because I can say that, during all my years at Spurs as both a player and captain, I saw here a partnership which worked beautifully and brought Tottenham more silverware.

When Nicholson brought Eddie in to join him on the coaching side, he made a smart move. What Bill had done was to form a coaching team: Bill would handle the technical side of things, while Eddie's strength was the basic skills.

Bill was aware of Eddie's enormous potential and, to be fair, Eddie did bring much to the table. But it must have been a challenge even to Eddie who, after all, was coming in to take charge of some of the game's biggest names – players who had won the Double just a few years earlier. So it was sink or swim for Baily. Bill threw him into the deep end. And luckily for Bill – he swam.

How did he swim? Let's look more closely at the positives in the Baily coaching style. First and foremost, he had the cockney front to stand up in front of the boys and be his natural, confident self. From the word go, he had a good rapport with the players. He was one of the lads. We all felt comfortable together. However, easily the best plus in Eddie's coaching was the fact that he had the skills to actually show you what he meant. In other words, when he talked about a skill, he could step in front of you and do it.

The difference between Bill and Eddie on the training pitch was that Bill could tell you how to volley, and Eddie could stand out in front of you and actually do it. He could volley the ball with fantastic accuracy, even though by then he was in his 40s and his knees and legs had gone.

When Eddie took us for sessions in the gymnasium, he would paint rings on the walls and we had to volley or pass the ball into the centre of them. Eddie would kick it off and every time he was 100 per cent accurate. That would impress the likes of Mackay, Chivers, Gilzean, etc. Bill could never do that sort of thing. With his photographic memory, Bill could explain tactics, but he wouldn't step up, grab a ball and give a riveting example as Eddie could.

Eddie had a wonderful coaching philosophy: 'If you are demonstrating a skill to top players and it works – DON'T do it again. The second time, you'll get it wrong and you won't impress the pupil.'

Eddie believed that the art of being a good coach was to demonstrate and quit while you were ahead!

Many years later, I remembered Eddie's tip when I took over as manager at Brighton. I was explaining to Tony Towner how he should run at the full-back, drop his shoulder, cut inside and fire the ball home high into the net. Tony tried to do it five times and couldn't master it. So I grabbed the ball and said to Tony, 'Look, let me show you.'

I took off my tracksuit top and off I went, charging at the full-back, dropping the shoulder, cutting inside and WHACK – the ball went into the net. By then, I was overweight and out of shape and I knew I couldn't do it again if asked. But Towner from then on always looked on it as something easy – even though it wasn't. Nine times out of ten, I would have got it wrong, but I quit while I was ahead: a lesson straight from the Eddie Baily master-class.

As an England player, Eddie showed brilliant skills, and these were to prove his ace card as he coached at Spurs. He lost his ability to run but he never lost his passing accuracy. He did it: we learnt. His ball-trapping was superb. Again, he would demonstrate it, but the skill we all enjoyed most was when he would pull a high ball out of the air and get it to sit on his foot. That would invariably draw a big round of applause from the lads, and that was how respect was built.

Bill, too, acknowledged Eddie's skill factor when he wrote in his *Glory Glory* book, 'Eddie Baily was an outstanding inside-forward and one of the greatest passers I have seen.'

Eddie too was very strong on knowing how to get the best out of certain players. If a player needed a rollicking to get him going, he would instigate it and then Bill would follow in. Eddie knew who to pick on. I have to say he mostly left me alone, but poor Martin Chivers would often come under fire.

Sometimes it worked, sometimes it didn't. Sometimes it went way over the top, and I remember having to step in and stick up for Chivers, whose game wasn't based on running himself into the ground. Chivers's philosophy was that for him to get the best results, he had to keep his energy for attacking play, especially when there was a race for the ball and a chance of scoring. He wanted to use all his energy on that and not on running up and down the pitch. That's how he was. It's fair to say that Eddie and Chivers didn't always see eye to eye, but Eddie had his coaching systems and by and large they worked.

It's appropriate to leave the last word on Eddie with Bill himself. It seems the great man had a deep-rooted respect for his assistant-manager's game and happily I can report he rated yours truly as well. Writing in his *Glory Glory* book, Bill is talking about Spurs' best team and he says, 'The candidates for the midfield positions are numerous. Ron Burgess has to be included and a choice would have to be made from Danny Blanchflower, John White, Glenn Hoddle, Ossie Ardiles, Eddie Baily, Martin Peters and Alan Mullery, all great players.'

Thanks, Bill. Eddie and I both take our hats off to you!

* * *

Eddie Baily and Ted Ditchburn, who played with Bill Nicholson in the famous push-and-run side, recalled those days when they talked to my co-author, Paul Trevillion. Mrs Ron Burgess also shared her memories with Paul, as did the acclaimed coach Dave Sexton, who watched Nicholson play from the Tottenham terraces:

Eddie Baily on Bill Nicholson

'I knew Bill for ten years as a player,' Baily tells us, 'and I worked with him for twelve years as his assistant-manager and coach. That's twenty-two years.

'As a player, Bill was never one of the boys. But he was, even then, a great club man. Bill was what I would call a very honest, very hard-working, never-let-you-down teammate, without having exceptional skill. He could tackle, head the ball, was an accurate passer and was rarely caught out of position, but he lacked real pace – he was never really quick. He jockeyed opponents very well and, with his exceptional quick reading of the game and football brain, his lack of pace was rarely exposed.

'Bill never liked playing against the ball-players like Jimmy Logie of

Arsenal, because they might turn him now and then, but Bill shouldn't have worried, because in the end he would get his foot in and upset them.

'I'll say this, and I know everyone in the push-and-run team would say the same, if Bill wasn't in the team on the pitch, you missed him, and you cannot pay a player a bigger compliment than that.'

Ted Ditchburn on Bill Nicholson

When I phoned Spurs goalkeeping legend Ted Ditchburn, I recognised his voice immediately. It was the same commanding voice that used to shout 'MINE' when he went for the ball and 'GET OUT, GET OUT, GET OUT' when his defenders fell back too close to his goal. Ditchburn, now in his 80s, apologised and said he was not up to a visit to talk about Bill Nicholson. He was waiting on a life-threatening heart operation.

Even so, when I asked him what stood out most when he played in goal behind Nicholson, he said, 'Bill was totally reliable. You could depend on Bill in every situation, because he always seemed to be there. When I was under pressure in a crowded goalmouth, when I came out of goal to get the ball and when I was looking for someone to throw the ball to, Bill was always available. I was also always very relieved when Bill had the ball; I knew he would never do anything silly. He was a great defender to have in front of you. Like I said, totally reliable and he was a great man to know.'

I thanked Ditchburn, and when I put the phone down I checked my scrapbook, which naturally, because Ditchburn was my hero, is full of newspaper cuttings and photographs of him when he was a player. Ditchburn was right: Nicholson was always reliable and available because, whether in close-up or in the distance, Nicholson can be easily recognised in nearly every action-shot picture of Ditchburn in the Spurs goalmouth.

WHO DID
RONNIE
BURGESS
SUCCEED AS
CAPTAIN, AND
WHICH SEASON
DID THIS
TAKE PLACE?

Ted Ditchburn

Ron Burgess

Alf Ramsey
Lilywhite magazine, 1953

Mrs Ron Burgess on Bill Nicholson

When the phone rang, I did not recognise the lady's voice on the line, but when she introduced herself as Mrs Ron Burgess, I was absolutely delighted – I had not expected the call.

Mrs Burgess was very apologetic when she explained that her husband Ron was very ill and in no fit shape to do an interview or even take a phone call and talk about his lifelong friend, Bill Nicholson.

She continued, 'I know Ron would have been overjoyed to talk about Bill. They were great friends. They joined the club together as young men. Ron always said they were great times and what a great player and teammate Bill was. He was also very proud of what Bill achieved as a manager. They always kept in touch – they never missed an opportunity to talk.'

She made it quite clear that if Ron had been able to take the phone call, he would have talked for hours about the wonderful friend and person Bill Nicholson was, and she was very sorry that Ron couldn't express these words himself.

I thanked her and put the phone down. I did not consider this a missed opportunity. In those few words, Mrs Ron Burgess had underlined the special relationship between the two men.

Sadly, three days later Ron Burgess passed away, but his dynamic captaincy and legendary presence at Tottenham Hotspur Football Club will never be forgotten.

Dave Sexton on Bill Nicholson

I was reading the Spurs 1961 Souvenir Brochure. It was the official publication of the Spurs players to mark their achievement in the season 1960–61. The distinguished and highly respected sports journalist Ken Jones had edited the brochure and wrote the 'pen pictures'. I had just read the one with the heading 'The Quiet Man', under which Bill Nicholson was talking about his days as a bright young Spurs hopeful:

> I had been with the club for almost four years, when one day I
> stopped in the middle of a game and realised that I had heard

the crowd roar for the very first time. I was so wrapped up in the game and so determined to keep working at my football that I had never noticed them before.

I always enjoyed everything Ken Jones wrote about Spurs. I enjoyed this piece on Nicholson, but I thought 'Four years? It must be a misprint! It should have read 'four weeks'. I decided to check it out the next time I saw Nicholson, and I did.

'Bill,' I said. 'I read you concentrated so hard during your early games, it was four years before you heard the noise of the crowd – was that right?'

'Who wrote that?' asked Nicholson.

'Ken Jones,' I replied.

'Then it's right.' Nicholson was walking away as he answered.

I never forgot that article or my brief conversation with Nicholson and it all came back when I was talking to Dave Sexton, one of the most highly regarded coaches and managers of the last 30 years, who is still with the FA helping the England coach Sven-Göran Eriksson.

'It was Nicholson's complete and absolute concentration which impressed me when I watched him play in the Tottenham push-and-run side,' Sexton told me. 'Because I lived in Chingford, it was easy for me to get to Tottenham on match days, so I was privileged to be able to watch a team full of internationals entertain and excite, playing fast, attacking, one-touch football which won matches in great style.

'The success of the free-scoring Arthur Rowe side was built on a well-organised and disciplined defence, and nobody was more organised or disciplined than Nicholson. He was an essential cog in that defensive system.

'Nicholson played his football with the minimum of fuss and the minimum of show. Everything he did in a game was with a purpose: never for a spectacular effect. Nicholson was a very disciplined defender. He never wandered out of position or strayed upfield; he was always on his guard not to leave space – a way open – a path to Ditchburn in the Spurs goal.

'His concentration throughout a match was intense. Nicholson never let up. There were no idle moments: not even when play was on the other side of the field, deep in the opposing half. Nicholson would be thinking, planning ahead, getting into position for the next move. When he got the ball, he would never hold on to it longer than necessary. He was always alert and aware of teammates in space, so he was able to knock a quick pass through the opposing defence before they had time to organise and cover up.

'Another of Nicholson's great strengths,' went on Sexton, 'was his fitness. He was never still. He was always on the move, being in position to cover his opponent and yet still being perfectly placed to help the centre-half, full-backs, even the goalkeeper, when they were in trouble.

'Nicholson at right-half had a great understanding with Alf Ramsey, who played at right-back. Very little got past these two. Ramsey, who was the automatic choice for England, would never head the ball if it was possible to get it under control with his chest or feet. He liked to play with the ball on the ground. On the occasions when the Spurs defence was under pressure, Ramsey radiated confidence with his cool, calm distribution of the ball in the tightest of spots. He was also a wonderful tactical passer, especially when hitting a long ball out of defence.'

As Sexton pointed out, the defence played a major role in that Tottenham team. I remembered that even the Spurs captain Ronnie Burgess, who was a human dynamo and the inspiration in midfield with his non-stop running and upfield surges, was, every season, good for five or six goals. But that was until Arthur Rowe pointed out his defensive duties in the push-and-run side. When Tottenham took the Second Division by storm, with an avalanche of goals, Burgess, for the first time in his career, completed a season without finding the back of the net once.

'The Tottenham attack was Walters, Bennett, Duquemin, Baily and Medley,' recited Sexton. 'They were all good, one-touch players. But the one I admired and really did enjoy watching was Eddie Baily. He was a magnificent first-time passer of a ball. He had the wonderful ability to be able to control the ball and pass it in one fluid movement – then he was off into position for the next move. Baily believed it was the second pass that did the damage to the opposition.'

Sexton was right. Spurs fans look back and talk about the attacking football and goals the push-and-run side scored, but as Sexton pointed out, what they seem to forget was the major part played by the defence. It was full of internationals. Nicholson and centre-half Harry Clarke were both capped, even if only the once. Ditchburn and Ramsey were England players. The captain and left-half Ronnie Burgess was an ever-present in the Welsh side and even Arthur Willis at left-back was capped by England. The defence was full of experience and backed up with considerable skill. It was the springboard for Tottenham's fast, attacking football.

The Tottenham defenders finished up with well over 70 caps between them, but oddly enough, the free-scoring Spurs forwards totalled less than 20 caps, and Baily got most of them.

Sexton looked back with fond memories and said, 'Right throughout my career as a player, manager and coach, both Nicholson and Baily were always willing to give me advice, discuss tactics or just talk about football. Never once were they too busy to talk to me. Baily, thank goodness, is still around, but sadly we have lost Nicholson. I will always remember Nicholson as a great player, a great coach and a great manager, but above all, I will remember him as a very kind man.'

CHAPTER FIVE

Greaves: The Goal-Scoring Genius

Jimmy Greaves's arrival at Tottenham was yet another example of Bill Nicholson at his most ruthless. It was 1961, Spurs had just done the Double and Les Allen had played a major role with 27 league and cup goals, many of them vital, including the winning goal against Sheffield Wednesday to clinch the league title. Surely Les's place was secure for another season. Or was it?

Well, no – not in Bill Nicholson's football world of perfection. For no sooner had Les put down his celebration glass of champagne, than was Bill urging the wonderful goal-scoring talents of Jimmy Greaves back to English football to wear a Spurs shirt. I always felt sorry for Les, who had done everything and more that could have been asked of him in that record-breaking Double side.

That was Bill's *modus operandi* in a nutshell. You are in a Double-winning side one year and next year you are out of the door! If Bill felt there were players out there who could make Spurs a better side, he would go out and buy them. As I say, Les had every reason to feel hard done by, but in hindsight you could understand Bill's thinking. It had to be an extra-special striker to make Bill get out his cheque book, and I am sure even Les would concede that Jimmy Greaves was just that.

Indeed, I would go as far as to say that Greaves was the best goal-

scorer I have ever seen. Certainly, at the time Bill signed him, he was as good as anyone in the world at scoring goals. He was averaging well over 30 a season: an unbelievable level of performance.

When I arrived at White Hart Lane in 1964, Jim had been at the club for three years. He left for West Ham in 1968, so I had the enviable privilege of playing in the same team as Jim for four years. The first thing I noticed about Jim was how laid back he was. He would sit in the team talks on a Friday smoking a pipe, totally cool and relaxed. His was a God-given talent if ever I have seen one, and he had the gift of being able to change the outcome of a match with one flash of brilliance. But genius comes at a price, and the price for Bill was that Jim wasn't going to knuckle down and play by Bill's rules. To Nicholson's credit, he accepted this and, as with Dave Mackay, if Jim delivered on the park, then Bill was happy to let him do things his own way.

Jim's way didn't include tackling players, didn't include chasing players to win the ball off them and didn't include running up and down the football pitch as a midfielder would. But it did include being clinical and lethal in front of goal and, if a chance presented itself, then Nicholson was never happier if the man it fell to was little Jim.

Jim had this wonderful ability over 10 yards to leave players for dead. Footballers like Frenchman Thierry Henry in later years would leave people for dead over 50 to 60 yards, but 'Greavsie' was a class above that. He would leave them for dead over *10* yards. A defender would be keeping pace with Jim and suddenly he would be off and away towards the goal. When he got there, you rarely saw him smash the ball into the net: he would prefer to side-foot the ball past the keeper. Jim would do this regularly week in and week out.

That was one side of Jim. The other side was his reaction to over-zealous defenders. Make no mistake, every time Jim pulled on a Spurs shirt he was a marked man. 'Stop Greaves and you stop Spurs' I am sure was often heard in the opposition dressing-room. That could mean only one thing: Jimmy was going to be closely marked and, if necessary, get a good kicking, and, sure enough, that happened just about every week. But to Jim's eternal credit he accepted it and never complained. He just picked himself up and got on with his job.

Jim did most of his work 30 yards from goal, where he would receive the ball, jink his shoulder and he was away. Then, inside the 18-yard box he was the sharpest operator I have ever seen. The ball was in the net. That was his job and Bill knew that. Bill didn't expect any more and, true to say, he never got it! Bill had to accept Jim as the great craftsman he was. His craft was scoring goals and, at the end of the day, that is what football is all about.

'You're only as good as your strikers' is a much-used saying in football and it explains why Bill Nicholson was willing to spend hours on a plane to Italy in 1961 in search of goal-scoring gold dust. Nicholson found it, paid the fee and brought Jimmy home, but, strange to say, if things had worked out differently when Jim was younger, Bill would not have needed to shell out a king's ransom. He so easily could have been a Spurs player from day one of his career. It is common knowledge that Bill saw a young Greaves play for London Schools at White Hart Lane and was very impressed by Jim's natural goal-scoring skills even then. All of London football, including Spurs boss Arthur Rowe, thought Jim was headed for Spurs, but it never happened. After much chitchat, Greaves decided on Stamford Bridge and a career with Chelsea, where most promising London lads headed.

I know that Bill had his theories as to why Tottenham would often lose the battle for schoolboy talent, chief among them being the fact that Spurs would never pay inducements to the mums and dads of exceptionally talented schoolboys. It is fair to say that in the early 1950s it was par for the course for parents to be given presents to help them to decide between one club and another. Lots of clubs had this policy, but Tottenham was one that didn't and at times it proved costly.

The irony of all this must have struck Bill when Jimmy made his debut for Chelsea against Spurs at White Hart Lane and notched his first league goal right there in front of him. It was a brilliant piece of individualism and a great strike: a Greavsie special.

'I wanted him from that moment on,' Bill was heard to say, years later.

Well, Bill finally got his man. But if you had said to Bill that day at the Lane that it would take a trip to Milan in Italy to land him, I am sure Bill would have said, 'I can't see that happening.'

But it did. Legend has it, and Nicholson did confirm it, that the deal was set in motion, in, of all places, the men's toilet at the Café Royal in Central London, where Jim and Bill were at a dinner and they both just happened to answer the call of nature at the same time. Over a light-hearted chat, Jim let it be known to Bill that he wouldn't mind a move to Spurs when he left AC Milan. Bill made a mental note as he adjusted his trousers. I have heard of spending a penny, but this particular trip to the gents was to cost Bill a whole lot more – £99,999, to be precise. It must rank as the most expensive toilet stop ever!

Not long after this chat, Jimmy starting hitting troubled times at AC Milan. He apparently had disagreements with their coach, the late Nereo Rocco. Bill remembered his little conversation with Jim in the gents. He stepped in, paid the £99,999 and brought Jim back to England.

But it wasn't that simple. Bill was involved in one of his toughest fights to land his man.

He later told me: 'The Greaves move from AC Milan was the most protracted of all my transfer dealings while I was at Tottenham. It went on and on and involved meetings in Milan, London and then finally Milan again, where I was head to head with Chelsea to get Jim's signature. I won the day; it was a real fight. But looking back it was all worth it. Jimmy did the business for me: he got Tottenham the goals.'

It wasn't all sweetness and light between Bill and Jimmy. I can remember several bust-ups between them and Jimmy would get furious with Bill. He would really have a go, but usually over very small things. Jimmy was never one to hold a grudge, so the next day it was all forgotten.

One side of Jim's life which he kept totally secret was his drinking. I certainly had no idea he had a problem in that area and I saw a lot of him. It wasn't until I read about it in the papers some years later that I learnt about his serious addiction to the booze. I know for a fact that Bill was as surprised as I was to hear about it. Even if Bill had known, my guess is that he would have adopted the same attitude as he did with Mackay – namely, that as long as it didn't interfere with his performance on the park, then he would turn a blind eye to it.

Bill told me that he never saw any tell-tale signs of heavy drinking in Jim's case and that if he had been drinking heavily, it certainly never affected his football. It seems he could take his booze, just as Mackay could. Every individual in football is different and Bill treated his players as adults who had to be trusted away from the game. He would never try to check up on his players once they left the ground. He would often tell us that the reputation of Tottenham Hotspur Football Club rested on our shoulders when we were out and would leave it at that.

From 1966 onwards, Jimmy's playing career at Spurs and England hit problems. He had a terrible run of bad luck. He got injured early in England's 1966 World Cup campaign and, by the time he had recovered full fitness, Geoff Hurst was established in the England side. Sir Alf Ramsey stuck with him, England won the World Cup and in the final Hurst was a hat-trick hero. It could so easily have been Jim and this must have hurt him terribly.

The next piece of bad luck came when Jim went down with hepatitis – a serious complaint for a footballer – and many felt, including Bill, that following that illness Jim's career started to go downhill. Basically, his reactions had lost their sharpness and he had started to slow down.

When Bill discovered that West Ham's Ron Greenwood fancied taking a chance with Greaves and that Martin Peters could be on offer, he didn't hesitate to do a deal and swap Greaves for Peters. On this occasion, unlike the Mackay transfer to Derby, Bill had reason to feel he called it right, for Jimmy lasted less than two seasons with West Ham before calling it a day. I think Greaves accepted that the genius needed to score goals was no longer at his disposal.

Talking of goals, let's end on a positive note. I am often asked what was the greatest goal I saw Jimmy score in a Spurs shirt. Let me try to describe it. We were playing Leicester City and Pat Jennings kicked the ball high into the air over the centre circle to where Greaves was standing. As it came down, he caught it on his instep and in the same movement swayed round to his left and Graham Cross of Leicester, who was bang up close to him, was left for dead. As Jimmy went round him, it was sheer poetry in motion. Then a midfield player came at him and Jim pushed the ball through the player's legs. Then he got to the last defender and he jinked past him. Now he only had the keeper to beat. The keeper went one way; Jim went round the other way. Then he stopped on the goal line and put his foot on the ball. He turned round, faced all the defenders and back-heeled the ball into the net! It was magic: pure genius.

* * *

My co-author, Paul Trevillion, covered Bill Nicholson's capture of Jimmy Greaves from AC Milan in his cartoon published in the *Tottenham Weekly Herald*. Here, Paul remembers a conversation he had with Bill about his Greaves–Nicholson cartoon and also reveals a classic Greaves–Nicholson story concerning Greaves's work rate, or lack of it!

Tottenham Weekly Herald, 1961

Freddie Cox on Jimmy Greaves

'I hope you are right.' It was the unmistakable voice of Bill Nicholson. I knew immediately he was referring to a cartoon I had drawn which had been published in the *Tottenham Weekly Herald*. It illustrated Jimmy Greaves kicking the ball with the caption 'If Greaves shows HALF the determination for getting goals – as Nicholson showed in getting him – watch out for fireworks'. I had drawn Bill Nicholson covered in sweat bubbles, carrying two suitcases with 'Milan' plastered all over them.

'Were you happy with your drawing, Bill?' I prompted him. I had been drawing cartoons for the *Tottenham Weekly Herald* and the Spurs *Lilywhite* magazine way back to the days when Nicholson was a player, and never once had he complimented me on one of my cartoons. Today was to be no exception.

'You'll never be able to draw Greaves covered in sweat bubbles,' laughed Nicholson. The conversation was over and Nicholson marched off.

In that brief exchange, I could tell, even though Nicholson had given me one of his rare laughs, that the sweat bubbles had hit a nerve. Nicholson liked his players to run and run and run. He liked them to *sweat*, but little Jim's goal-scoring genius both in and around the box was not dependent on him shedding one little drop.

It was November 1971, ten years to the day since I'd had the 'sweat bubble' conversation with Nicholson, and I was now talking to Freddie Cox. I've always liked Cox, dating back to the '40s, when I collected his autograph. He always signed, and I enjoyed watching him play on the right-wing for Tottenham in the side that included Nicholson, Ditchburn and Burgess. Cox was a great striker of the ball. He didn't score many goals, but those that went in were usually spectacular – ones you remembered.

I was working on my article for the *Sunday People* and I was picking the astute footballing brain of Cox, who was the manager when Bournemouth signed Ted MacDougall. It had proved an inspired signing, as MacDougall was now rattling in goal after goal and earning comparisons with Greaves.

'How do you compare MacDougall with Greaves?' I asked Cox.

'Every forward has the equipment to put the ball in the net,' explained Cox. 'They can all kick and head the ball. But that equipment counts for nothing if you're not in the right place at the right time to use it. This is where MacDougall is like Greaves: he's there in position to snap up half-chances, rebounds and things like that. If the penalty area was divided up into 20 squares, MacDougall, like Greaves, would always be in the one the ball bounced in.'

The more Cox talked about MacDougall, the more I realised I had a great piece, and when it appeared in the newspaper that Sunday, there was a one-word banner headline on the back page of the *Sunday People* which spelt out: 'MacDougoal'. Bournemouth had beaten Margate 11–0 in the first round of the FA Cup and MacDougall had scored *nine* of the goals: a record for an FA Cup game.

I phoned Cox on the Monday and complimented him on his timing. We had a good laugh and Cox especially liked the MacDougoal play on words.

'Do we have another Jimmy Greaves?' I asked Cox.

'To compare MacDougall with Greaves would be wrong,' replied Cox. 'Greaves had a style all his own. He was unique: a one-off. Greaves made goal-scoring look easy. It was effortless: a stroll in the park. Greaves never broke sweat.'

With that, I jumped in and told Cox the Nicholson 'covered with sweat bubbles' episode when he signed Greaves.

'So that's where the Nicholson–Greaves after-match shirt story originated.'

'What story was that?' I asked Cox.

'The after-match shirts – the sweat. You must know it,' came back Cox.

But this was one Tottenham story that had escaped me, so I asked Cox to tell it.

'The story goes,' began Cox, 'when the Tottenham players came into the dressing-room after a game, Nicholson would go round and feel their shirts to check they were soaked in sweat. He would go up to every Tottenham player and very soon his hand was dripping wet, but always he left Jimmy Greaves until last.'

I said, 'Why was that?'

Cox laughed, 'He used to dry his hands on Jimmy's shirt!'

CHAPTER SIX

Mackay: Nicholson's Best Buy

Let me put my cards on the table. Dave Mackay was the best all-round footballer I have ever seen and I've seen a few. In fact, as an England and Fulham player I had the doubtful privilege of marking Pelé on several occasions and I am proud to say he never scored against me in open play. But having played against the great man I still wouldn't hesitate in putting Mackay at the very top of my list. He was certainly one of the hardest and fiercest competitive footballers I have watched or played with. He would make today's so-called hard men look absolute softies.

Bill Nicholson never did a better job than the day he brought Mackay to White Hart Lane. Bill went on record and said that Dave was his best-ever buy. I am sure he was. He was your real-life Roy of the Rovers. He could play in every position in the team, including goal, where he was a fabulous performer.

When I arrived at Tottenham in 1964, Dave was recovering from a broken leg. But even then I could see why this fierce warrior was such an out-and-out winner. He was totally determined to get back into shape and the way he pounded up and down the terraces as he strengthened the muscles in his legs was awesome to see. A little thing like a broken leg wasn't going to put a dampener on Dave's career, that was for sure.

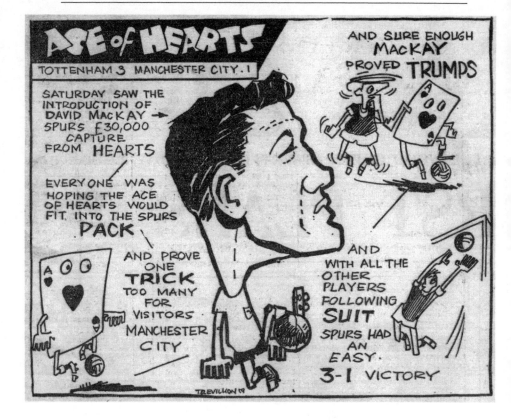

Tottenham Weekly Herald, 1959

Dave hated losing at anything. He would work hard to keep ahead of the pack and he would do all sorts of challenging skill tricks to keep that competitive edge sharp. I saw him throw a coin in the air and catch it on his foot, transfer it to his other foot, then flick it up so it landed on his forehead, then let it run down his nose and then finally let it drop into his top pocket. I have seen him control an orange with his feet and keep it up in the air for ages. The man had all the skill and technical ability, yet at the same time was a totally fearless ball winner. He had the lot.

Nicholson knew this only too well and he wasn't prepared to upset the apple-cart in any way. Everyone at the club knew that Dave enjoyed a drink or two after a game and Bill was more than happy to go along with this as long as Dave did the business on the park. I can remember the time I was in Bill's office one Tuesday morning and saw this enormous pile of letters on his desk.

'Goodness, what are all those about?' I enquired.

'Oh,' Bill replied, 'they are all from Tottenham fans telling me they saw Dave out on the town over the weekend.'

'How do you deal with them?' I further enquired.

With that, Bill stood up and, with a grand flourish with his arm, he swept the entire pile of letters into his bin. That, for me, said it all.

Nicholson knew that Mackay's presence was vital if Spurs were to continue as a major force in English football. Dave was my skipper during my early years at the club and as a Spurs new boy I could sense Dave's influence in all areas and not only during a match. At our training ground at Cheshunt, his very presence would have an uplifting and very positive effect on the whole squad. He was a born leader and just being there inspired other players. He was, indeed, the heart and soul of the Tottenham team.

It all started on 17 March 1959: that was the day Bill never forgot. He paid Hearts £32,000 (the highest ever fee paid for a half-back in Britain at the time) and Mackay was his. It was a culmination of several months' patient work by Bill, who had been on Mackay's trail for weeks and had been initially told the player wasn't available by Hearts boss Tommy Walker. But Nicholson persisted. Walker eventually had a change of mind and in stepped Bill.

Every great manager needs a slice of luck and this was a transfer where Lady Luck smiled on Bill. His original choice as a midfield player was Mel Charles of Swansea, but Bill decided to push on for Mackay because Charles at that time was injured. This injury undoubtedly changed the history of Tottenham Hotspur Football Club. Although I am sure Bill was excited by his new Scottish capture, I am sure he could never have envisaged that, just two short years later, Mackay would be the pivotal player in clinching the record-breaking Double.

However, it is fair to say the early signs were promising, especially on the training ground. I can remember how shocked I was by the ferocity of Dave's commitment in the practice games when I joined from Fulham, where the entire training experience was in a lower key. The six-a-side games at Spurs were an all-out war, with no holds barred, and it was the explosive Mackay who set the tone.

It was this competitive spirit that served us so well come Saturday afternoon. We had been in hard-fought games all week at our training ground thanks to Dave's unquenchable desire to win. Saturday was just a continuation of our training – minus the really dirty stuff. Looking back, the sad thing for me was that I never once got on the same side as Dave in those six-a-side games and that meant only one thing: when we clashed, we would literally kick lumps out of each other! Nicholson saw to it that there were no rules, so there was fouling, pushing and fighting and it was inevitable that Dave and I would come face to face and scuffles would follow. This was none of your 'handbags at ten paces' stuff. Dave would kick me and I would retaliate and often it got very nasty, but that was the nature of the training session. Winning was the aim, but it was all smiles afterwards and nobody had a bigger smile on their face than Nicholson.

Because of Mackay's fierce, domineering attitude to life, one might wonder did he have any respect for anyone, let alone Nicholson? Well, the answer is that their relationship was a great one. Bill knew what a diamond he had in Mackay and dealt with him accordingly. Yes, in Dave's case he made allowances, but any shrewd soccer boss would and Bill was shrewd, very shrewd. He allowed Mackay plenty of rope and it paid off. A great bond and a great relationship developed between the two of them. It was one built on respect, and Mackay respected Nicholson, but he didn't fear him. Dave Mackay feared no one!

Bill very wisely didn't bother himself too much with Mackay's life away from football, and what a good decision that was. It would have almost certainly led to a nasty clash. Mackay lived for football and Tottenham. He also enjoyed a pint or two, and that's putting it mildly.

Deep down, Bill loved the man. I remember when Mackay broke his leg for the second time in a reserve-team game I was sitting in the front of the coach close to Bill when he was told the news and I could see he was visibly shaken and very upset. I remember how surprised I was, as Bill never showed his feelings, but he was close to tears and, at that moment in that little corner of the coach, I caught a brief glimpse of just how much Nicholson loved his Scottish superstar. No other player, during my time at the club, would have drawn that reaction from Nicholson.

I always measured Dave's toughness by his broken-legs track record.

No injury scares a footballer more than a broken leg, for without your legs you have no career in football; you are finished. Yet Dave suffered two broken legs and bravely fought his way back twice to lead Spurs to more glory, culminating in him being the captain and leading the side to victory in the 1967 FA Cup final. That took some serious guts and determination from Mackay.

In the Cup final itself, Dave didn't stand out in the game, but to the Tottenham players he was everything, because he was such an inspirational leader. On the pitch, he was doing Nicholson's job as manager, which was just what Bill asked him to do. Nicholson was happy for Dave to take the double role, because he could see the players respected him and they would take notice of him.

Nicholson had his idea of when a player was past his peak and, in the summer of 1968, he made his decision that Mackay no longer figured in his Tottenham plans. I can still picture the scene clearly. It happened on the day we returned for pre-season training. At lunch that day there were Dave Mackay and Brian Clough deep in talks at one end of the table, with Bill Nicholson and Eddie Baily and the Tottenham staff sitting at the other end. Everyone knew that Cloughie was there to sign Dave and the Spurs players just couldn't believe it. Dave was on his way and Clough had his man for as little as £5,000.

This was the ruthless side of Nicholson. He could and would act with no respect for a person's feelings if he felt a player had passed his peak, and it didn't matter who it was. With Mackay, he had made up his mind and that was that. In hindsight, it is now possible to wonder whether he got that one right. Did he underestimate the fighting qualities of Dave Mackay, the man he believed had left his best days behind him?

As it turned out, Cloughie was picking up a bargain with plenty of mileage still left on the clock. When Dave moved to Derby County, they were a Second Division side, but after Dave's arrival that all changed. In his first season, they were promoted to the old First Division and that meant one thing – a Derby v. Spurs clash was certain for the next season. Having got to know Dave quite well, I am sure he was licking his lips and thinking, 'I'll show Bill Nicholson I'm not over the hill.'

When the big day arrived, we travelled to Derby's Baseball Ground, knowing that Dave would be waiting with something special up his

Tottenham Weekly Herald, 1963

sleeve. I remember it was a mud heap of a pitch and, as Spurs skipper, I walked up to the centre of the ground to spin the coin. Mackay was the Derby captain and, as I shook hands with him, I said, 'Dave, it's really lovely to see you.'

He snapped back at me: 'We're going to stuff you this afternoon. I mean, STUFF YOU.'

Derby played us off the park and beat us 5–0, and Mackay was the best player on the pitch. He proved his point to Nicholson that afternoon and I am sure he must have made Bill think long and hard as he made his way back to London.

I recently had a look at the Derby v. Spurs home programme on that Saturday, 20 September 1969, and I noticed that it cost just a shilling in old money. My, those were the days, I can hear you say! Turning inside, I came across Brian Clough's column, and he had this to write about the game:

> Today we welcome Tottenham, who for so long have been among the cream in the First Division. It will be nice to do well, so that we can pay a little bit back to Dave Mackay for what he has done for us.

Well, Clough's boys certainly didn't let him down. On that day, they played out of their skins. They were terrific.

Delving deeper into the programme, I saw that Dave himself also had something to say about the match. It's a lot more polite than what he said to me in the centre circle before the game. Dave writes:

> Today is a wonderful day for me. When I left Spurs, not much more than a year ago, I suppose I must have wondered whether I would ever play against them or whether I would ever play in a match with Jimmy Greaves and all the others.
>
> Now, not only am I playing against them, but they are the underdogs. What an amazing situation! I only hope that I am as happy tonight as I was at five o'clock last Saturday after our great win at Newcastle. There is no room for sentiment in sport. I suppose I will always have a soft spot for Spurs, but I don't like to think of them doing us out of two points today!

The line-up of the two teams brings back some wonderful memories. For Tottenham, we had Pat Jennings in goal, Phil Beal and Cyril Knowles as full-backs, myself, Mike England and Peter Collins as half-backs and a forward line which read: Martin Chivers, Jimmy Greaves, Alan Gilzean, John Pratt and Roger Morgan. Sub was Tony Want. Derby lined up like this: Les Green, Ron Webster, John Robson, Alan Durban, Roy McFarland, Dave Mackay, John McGovern, Willie Carlin, John O'Hare, Kevin Hector, Alan Hinton and sub Frank Wignall.

How did Derby react to their astonishing 5–0 triumph? Well, not surprisingly, in their home match programme dated Wednesday, 24 September 1969, they had plenty to say. Even their chairman, Sydney Bradley, wanted to make a comment about the thrashing we took. He wrote:

> The match against Newcastle fades from the limelight after last Saturday's brilliant success against the Spurs. What a real soccer thrill this was. As one newspaper writes, Derby have everything, 'disciplined and tough at the back, intelligent and decisive in midfield, penetrative and packed with power up front'. What a great day it was for our skipper Dave Mackay; the 'Boys' certainly turned it on for him, and I am sure it will be a match he will always remember.

What, I wondered, did Dave himself make of it all? Well, as I fingered my way through the pages of the old programme, I soon found out. Dave writes:

> What, really, can I add to all the things that have been said about our great win over Spurs last Saturday? Perhaps the only thing I would like to emphasise is that I am not gloating over the fact that it was Spurs who we thrashed.
>
> I was glad because we won 5–0, but no more pleased than if it had been anybody else on the receiving end. I had several very happy years with Spurs and there is no question of 'revenge' on my part when I play against them.

Dave may have said that he wasn't gloating over the fact that it was

Spurs on the receiving end of such a hammering, but knowing at first hand the competitive attitude that Dave had to life, I am sure that somewhere in a tiny corner, at the back of his mind, he must have entertained a thought along the lines of, 'That, Mr Nicholson, shows you there was a lot more fuel left in the tank when you sold me.' Dave loved to prove people wrong, as he did throughout his career, especially the doubters who said he would never come back from two broken legs.

People often ask me if I question Bill's judgement over Mackay and the answer is always the same: 'no'. I have never done that because Bill had his track record to hold up in front of you. Over the years, he got more things right than he did wrong. When it came to players, Nicholson had absolutely no sentimentality. There was just no room for it in his Tottenham world. If he believed a player was past his prime as far as winning silverware was concerned, he would let him go. He did it with me after I had played in the 1972 Spurs side which won the 1972 UEFA Cup. He also did the same with Jimmy Greaves when he let him go to West Ham. His attitude was always the same: 'Thanks, but it's time to go.'

Mackay went on to do well for Cloughie, and Nicholson's rebuilding job after Dave left in July 1968 gathered pace. Come the 1970–71 season, Bill had the League Cup for his trophy room.

Between 1964 and 1968, Dave and I got to know each other very well and my admiration for him was immeasurable. I learnt a lot from his captaincy methods and how he hated to lose. I never saw him nervous before a game. He was always noisy and positive and would walk round clenching his fist. When he patted you on the back, it was never a gentle touch but a really hard WHACK, which made sure you were wide awake before you got out on the pitch. A certain amount of Dave's attitudes became my attitudes when I took over as skipper from Mackay in 1968. It was, in a way, business as usual. Alan Mullery was Dave Mackay in many ways; it was just a continuation of what Mackay had been doing and I am sure Nicholson had planned it that way when he made me captain. He knew I was making his life much easier, because I was capable of leading both on and off the pitch.

Mackay, of course, will always be remembered for his role in the 1961 Double team when he played under the captaincy of Danny Blanchflower, but the major part he played in that history-making side was recognised by Nicholson when he said, 'Mackay probably did more than anyone to forge a team capable of winning the Double.' Having seen Mackay close up and having played with him, I can well understand what Nicholson meant: the man was a human powerhouse.

* * *

At the London launch of the National Association of Boys' Clubs' (NABC) annual fundraising week on 17 October 1988, my co-author, Paul Trevillion, a great admirer of Graeme Souness, talked to him and discovered there was a softer side to Nicholson. The event was held at the prestigious Insurance Hall in the City of London, where more than 2,000 boys of the NABC and many famous stars of sport were present, including Sir Roger Bannister, Sir Henry Cooper, Steve Davis, Frank Bruno and John Conteh. Graeme Souness recalled his early days at Tottenham with Bill Nicholson while in conversation with Paul that day – early days which included cleaning my boots. Let me explain in more detail:

Alan Mullery on Souness and Nicholson

There is no better example than what happened with Graeme Souness to show the other side of the dour, even tough public image which was the Nicholson hallmark. In the case of Souness, Bill Nicholson showed genuine concern and deep understanding for a player's feelings, because basically, out of the goodness of his heart, he let Souness, who was homesick, return to Scotland. Bill showed a fatherly understanding with the very unhappy Souness and I know Graeme was always deeply grateful for that.

Souness had come down from Scotland and was another of a long line of Scottish talent that Bill had got his hands on. He was only a teenager and I remember he was in digs quite near the Spurs ground. One of his first duties at Tottenham, would you believe, was to clean my boots! I would give him a little cash tip for his troubles, because he always did a good job, and now, whenever we see each other we always enjoy a good laugh and a joke about that time.

Souness had few opportunities to make the Spurs first team, but I do clearly remember him coming onto the field on one of our European trips. I was hauled off when we were well ahead and Souness was allowed to sample European football for about 20 minutes. I need no reminding of the eagerness he showed when he ran past me onto the pitch. He was full of confidence, even brash, and showed with almost his first touch why Bill thought so highly of him. He lacked nothing as a player.

But Bill took pity on him and allowed him to return home to Scotland. This must have been very hard for Bill because he rated Souness very highly. He believed he could take over from Mackay. But Souness, thanks to Nicholson, went to Middlesbrough, because it was much nearer his home in Scotland than London. It was a major loss for Spurs. Souness would have eventually challenged me and Steve Perryman and, with his exceptional talent plus his physical commitment, he would definitely have made his mark in the Spurs first team.

Bill never mentioned Souness to me again after he left and he didn't need any Souness reminders. Souness moved on from Middlesbrough to Liverpool, won five league titles, three European Cups, four League Cups and topped it off with fifty-four international caps for Scotland – reason even for Nicholson never to mention Souness's name again. But Souness is always the first to admit that it was an unbelievably kind gesture of Bill's to let him go home and I know Graeme appreciated it then and still appreciates it now.

CHAPTER SEVEN

Bill's Volatile Relationship with Blanchflower

On the outside, to most of the fans of the Tottenham Double-winning side of 1961, it appeared that captain Danny Blanchflower and manager Bill Nicholson had a relationship as smooth as the sea on a calm summer day. In fact, it was anything but. I would describe their relationship as volatile, mainly because Danny was always inquisitive. He would constantly query Bill on techniques, tactics and ploys, etc.

I gleaned nearly all of my Blanchflower–Nicholson insights by talking to Bill and Danny over the years and not from playing alongside Danny – indeed, it was injuries to Blanchflower and Mackay that led to me landing up at White Hart Lane. Blanchflower had a cartilage operation, which today would be relatively straightforward, but, being back in those days, it finished his career. The result was my arrival to help try to fill the holes left by these two giants of Tottenham.

Although, as I say, I never had the chance to play in the same team as Danny, I would often talk to Bill about the articulate Northern Irishman. And then in the late '70s when I was manager of Brighton, Danny would make yearly visits to see me at the South Coast club in his role as football writer on the *Sunday Express*. Those were always memorable occasions, as, in the main, after a brief chat about

Brighton, I listened to Danny pour out his mighty football wisdom and experiences.

From all my chats with Nicholson and Blanchflower and members of the Double side, it appears that there was always a bone of contention between them and it was nearly always about tactics. For example, when the Tottenham goalkeeper, Bill Brown, had the ball in his hands, Blanchflower would drop back and collect the ball off him, 20 yards out. But Nicholson didn't want Blanchflower to do this.

A typical conversation would go like this:

> Nicholson: I don't want you to drop back – I want you to get the ball further up the field.
>
> Blanchflower: Yes, fine – but I've got to get up there and we might not get possession of the ball. At least, doing it my way, we always get possession.
>
> Nicholson: I agree, Danny, but not outside our own penalty box.
>
> Blanchflower: Yes, but my way we have still got possession and we haven't given the ball away.
>
> Nicholson: Agreed, but at times you will. I don't want you dropping back to pick up the ball from the goalkeeper when the two full-backs have moved well upfield with the centre-half. What's the point in you running back to the goalkeeper and picking the ball up there? When it is knocked forward, you now have to run 80 yards to get up the field.
>
> Blanchflower: No, I don't agree. My way means we always have possession of the ball.

This is how they would carry on and on and on. They both believed they were right. But in the end, Bill would always win because he was the manager.

I would love to have been a fly-on-the-wall at some of the Blanchflower–Nicholson 'discussions', because Danny could talk the hind leg off a donkey. When Danny was in full flow, it was almost impossible to stop him. I can imagine Nicholson finding it hard to get a word in edgeways – apart from the crucial one at the end. But, as I say, Bill was the manager; he was always right; he always had the last word.

I can remember the first season I was at Brighton. We got promotion from the old Third Division to the Second and Blanchflower phoned me and said, 'Alan, do you mind if I come down and see you to do an article on you and Brighton?'

'Of course you can, Danny. We'd love to see you,' I replied eagerly, as I was only too pleased to get some national recognition for the club, plus I knew Danny would be full of all the latest football gossip.

Blanchflower said, 'I'll be getting the train down from London. Any chance of somebody picking me up from Brighton station?'

'Yeah,' I told him. 'I'll pick you up, Danny, no trouble.'

From Brighton station to the old Goldstone Ground was about six minutes by car on a good day and, as I drove, Danny talked to me about Brighton and what I had achieved. And that was the only airtime I got! For the next three hours, he talked about Danny Blanchflower and what he had done at Tottenham. Brighton and Hove Albion Football Club was never mentioned again! So you can see, I got a pretty good insight into the Blanchflower–Nicholson relationship.

On subsequent visits, Danny would cover a whole range of other football subjects: how he would change the game, how he would do this and that. Danny could talk a fantastic game, but he also played a fantastic game. It was during these trips that I could see just why he could drive Nicholson completely crackers, as he did on occasions. But despite Danny's non-stop talking, I know that deep down Nicholson loved the man. To achieve what these two did, there had to be a deep bond of respect and love and it was there in extra large dollops.

I still have a chuckle about Blanchflower's visits to Brighton, because despite just six minutes' conversation in total devoted to the club, he still managed to write some terrific lengthy articles on us. Danny would tell me, 'Alan, you want to get rid of so and so,' or, 'I wouldn't keep him.'

I would reply, 'Is that right, Dan? When did you last see Brighton play?'

'Oh, I haven't seen you play live this season,' said Danny. 'Just seen you on TV.'

But Blanchflower clearly did his homework on us, because his *Sunday Express* articles were always bang on the button – a great read.

This was the Blanchflower that Nicholson had to work with and my firm impression was that Nicholson would have listened to Blanchflower on the training ground, but off it maybe not quite so much.

At the time of going to press
DANNY BLANCHFLOWER
remains on the " for sale "
list. But Tottenham are well
in the market and it is likely
he will join the famous
London club.

Weekly Sporting Review &
Showbusiness, 1954

I am sure that one reason why Bill and Danny had such a close bond was the fact that when Nicholson stopped playing for Spurs in the mid-'50s it was Blanchflower who was brought in by Arthur Rowe to replace him. Rowe paid Aston Villa £30,000 to capture Blanchflower, then 29 years old, in a bidding war with Arsenal.

Nicholson was appointed club coach, so his working relationship with Blanchflower began at once. It was a time of massive change at the club and soon after a disastrous FA Cup exit, at the hands of York City, Arthur Rowe quit and Jimmy Anderson moved into the hot seat. Immediately, he made Blanchflower club captain.

Not surprisingly, Blanchflower was a controversial skipper, and there were numerous clashes between Blanchflower and boss Anderson. Blanchflower lost the job and various other players had a crack at it. Harry Clarke, Tony Marchi, John Ryden and even Bobby Smith had their turns as captain.

In October 1958, Anderson called it a day and Nicholson was appointed manager. Tottenham made a great start. They beat Everton 10–4, but the four goals conceded did not please Nicholson and the seeds of his volatile relationship with Blanchflower were sown at once. Nicholson was quick to name Blanchflower as one of the weak links in defence. To his credit, Blanchflower took the criticism on board and played it more Nicholson's way.

But it still wasn't good enough for Nicholson. Early in 1959, Nicholson dropped Blanchflower for a series of games, all of which Tottenham won, and Blanchflower had seen enough. He demanded a transfer. Nicholson wouldn't allow it.

Bill told me later, 'Danny took it well. I knew I could have a sensible chat with Danny without him storming off in a huff. He listened and he understood why. I had told him there was no way he was going to leave Tottenham. To be honest, I was well aware he was a leader of men and I still had it in my mind to make him captain.'

In March of that year, Nicholson made one of his best decisions. He appointed Danny Blanchflower as captain again. Danny replaced Bobby Smith, who wasn't comfortable as skipper. Two years later, Danny led Spurs to the historic Double. And that Double was something I heard a lot about from Blanchflower during his memorable trips to Brighton. He loved remembering the build-up to

Tottenham Weekly Herald,
1958

the Double, and he told me that, as early as 1958, he was telling the likes of Stan Cullis and Joe Mercer that he believed the Double could be done and that Spurs would be the team to do it.

That may not sound much now, but in those days, the Double was regarded as 'not on'. Many teams had got close, but failed, so it was generally accepted in football circles that it couldn't be done in modern times. Danny was alone in predicting that it was possible. He loved having dreams like that. He was that sort of a man. He also knew that he and Bill were quietly and quickly building an extraordinary side at White Hart Lane. And, most importantly in Danny's mind, he was at the centre of all the glamour and the action.

I wasn't fully aware of just how important a figure Blanchflower was in that 1961 Double side until he told me over one of our many leisurely lunches at Hove's Courtlands Hotel how he could change the rhythm and pace of the game. Danny explained to me, 'I had the ball more often than any other player in that 1961 team, so I made sure I made good use of it.'

But what really struck me during my Brighton talks with Blanchflower was just how similar his views on the game were to Nicholson's. This surely was the magic chemistry which powered Bill and Danny to that Double. Nicholson believed winning wasn't enough – you had to do it with style. And Blanchflower saw things exactly like that as well.

Blanchflower would tell me, 'Alan, football is not entirely about winning, or even goals, or breathtaking saves or die-hard supporters – it's about glory. It's about performing in style, having a bit of a flourish in everything you do.'

When Blanchflower spoke like that, I always believed it could have been Nicholson talking.

Indeed, on one famous night in Rotterdam in May 1963, it was Blanchflower's talking that many feel led to Tottenham becoming the first British side to lift a European trophy. They were playing Atletico Madrid in the final of the European Cup-Winners' Cup. Tottenham did not have Mackay, due to illness, and Blanchflower himself was not 100 per cent fit thanks to a knee injury. For once, Nicholson was struggling for words in the team talk before the game. Mackay's absence was clearly playing heavily on his mind. Nicholson decided to spell out how good Atletico were, and in doing so failed to lift the troops. Once Nicholson had left the dressing-room, Blanchflower stood up and enjoyed his finest moment as Spurs captain.

He got his magic tongue in full gear and gave the pep talk of his life, getting the boys to feel 10-ft tall and ready to beat the world. They marched out with Blanchflower's words ringing in their ears and won 5–1.

However, it would be totally unfair on Bill for Blanchflower to get all the credit for one of the greatest days in Spurs history. Many thought that Tottenham's best player that night was little Terry Dyson, and Dyson himself has revealed that it was Bill who took him and Cliff Jones to one side just before the team went out and said, 'This will be your night. Take on the full-backs as often as you can. You can beat them.'

Bill was spot-on. His words of encouragement clearly worked. After 16 minutes, Jones crossed and Greaves put Spurs ahead, and Dyson went on to play the game of his life, scoring two great goals.

Between them, Danny, who was by this time also acting as Bill's assistant-manager, had coached one of the best ever performances out of a Tottenham team and legend has it that the celebrations that night in Rotterdam continued into the early hours of the morning and even included a rare visit by Bill himself. That, indeed, I would have loved to have seen. It is a measure of how much pleasure Bill got out of that victory. It was what he always wanted: a big win in a final and all done with a swagger and a bit of true Tottenham style.

But Nicholson's admiration for Blanchflower went deeper than that night in Rotterdam. When I was leading the Tottenham team, Bill would often talk to me about Danny and I knew Bill felt that he was never quite able to emulate the magical, intimate relationship he had with Danny with any of his other captains, especially when it came to discussing the team and the tactics. I know that Bill missed it.

During my time at Tottenham, Bill would suddenly mention Danny at one of our team talks. This nearly always happened if we were failing to do something that Danny had been brilliant at. I remember Bill would tell us, 'Danny would have done it this way. I want you now to do what Danny did.' That shows the depth of Nicholson's admiration for his Double-winning captain. Blanchflower's influence lived on at White Hart Lane long after he hung up his boots.

I always did my best with Bill, but what he had with Danny was extra-special: a once-in-a-lifetime experience. As Bill often said to me, 'I loved talking with Danny – he was such a great chat merchant, but he was also *some* player as well, and, despite our occasional differences, he was a magnificent captain with an exceptional football brain. He played his part and I am very proud of the achievements of that Tottenham team that Danny led to glory in the early '60s.'

* * *

BLANCHFLOWER

AT 37, DANNY BLANCHFLOWER IS THE OLDEST PLAYER IN THE SPURS TEAM. HE WAS TWICE VOTED "FOOTBALLER OF THE YEAR" — A RECORD HE SHARES WITH TOM FINNEY. BORN IN BELFAST, THIS SLIGHTLY BUILT RIGHT HALF RECEIVED ALL HIS EARLY FOOTBALL TRAINING FROM HIS MOTHER.

Glasgow Evening Citizen, 1962

And what manager played a key role in helping Bill Nicholson clinch that historic Double in 1961? It was none other than the Liverpool legend, Bill Shankly. Here, my co-author, Paul Trevillion, reveals the full story:

Bill Shankly on Bill Nicholson

I was sitting in Don Revie's office in the Leeds United football club. It was 1972. Revie never took phone calls when I was in the room, but this was an exception and he was in full flow, talking about the match Leeds had played that previous Saturday. Between laughs, he kept repeating the name 'Bill'. My first reaction was that he was talking to Bill Nicholson, but the repeated Revie laugh, out of place in a Nicholson conversation, had me second-guessing, and when the name 'Liverpool' was mentioned, I knew it must be Bill Shankly on the other end of the line.

'I've got Paul Trevillion in my office,' laughed Revie. 'Now you can tell him how, if it wasn't for you, Bill, Tottenham would never have won the Double.'

Revie went to hand me the phone, but Shankly hadn't finished. 'Bill,' said Revie, 'tell him that as well. But Hunter is still a harder tackler than Smith,' insisted Revie.

They were mentioning a football article I had illustrated in the *Sunday People*, claiming Hunter was a harder tackler than Smith because he left the bigger bruises.

Revie put the phone in my hand. He then held up ten fingers, pointed to his watch and walked out of the room. Revie was well rehearsed: when I was given the opportunity, I could talk all day on Tottenham. Revie had made it clear I had only ten minutes with Shankly, so I dived straight in.

'What part did you play in Tottenham winning the Double?' I questioned.

'Everything,' roared back Shankly, 'EVERYTHING. Nicholson has me to thank for the Double. I won it for him and I tell him that every time we meet. Bill just shakes his head but he knows I'm right, even though he will never admit it. Bill quickly changes the subject and then has a go back at me. But he knows I'm right.'

But what did Shankly do, I wanted to know. I decided to press the point, but before I could get the words out: 'Terry Dyson,' Shankly shouted down the phone. 'TERRY DYSON!' he repeated even louder. 'Bill wanted Denis Law when I had him at Huddersfield. He offered me Terry Dyson, Dave Dunmore and cash. It was a good deal. I thought about it. But Dyson and Dunmore . . . two reserves for Law. I wanted a Tottenham first-team player, but Nicholson wouldn't have it. Dyson, Dunmore and cash was the deal and Nicholson kept urging me to take it. He kept telling me what a great job Dyson, a Yorkshire lad, would do for Huddersfield. Bill insisted it was only because he had Medwin and Jones (Welsh internationals), that Dyson wasn't in the first team.

'"Dyson's a little tiger," said Bill. "He's brave, never stops running, pops up everywhere, upsets the opposition and he scores goals."

'I said, "Bill, he's a midget. He's only 4-ft tall. He never heads the ball."

'Nicholson came straight back: "Dyson is 5 ft 3 in. and he scores with his head."

'"Bill," I said, "Dyson's 5-ft tall when he's wearing football boots with extra-high studs. He's a midget."

'Bill would have none of it. "He's a little tiger. He's a great little player. Dyson's a match-winner."

'Nicholson was a very good judge of a player. It was obvious he rated Dyson very highly, and the more he talked the more I was tempted. I must admit I was very tempted. But Denis Law? No – I couldn't let Denis Law go for two reserves. So I held out. It was a first-team Tottenham player or no deal. Nicholson put the phone down. Dyson was still a Tottenham player and I still had Law.'

Before I could put another question to Shankly, he motored on. He was living up to his reputation as the best talker in the business.

'In trying to convince me how good Dyson was, Nicholson now realised what a valuable player he had in him; he was one to keep. Nicholson didn't try to sell him again. By not taking Dyson off Nicholson's hands, I had done him the biggest of all favours. Twelve months later, Dyson was in the Tottenham team and he was the one who won them the Double. He scored nearly 20 goals to win them the league. He was one of the few players who performed on the day when they beat Leicester 2–0 to win the Cup. He set up Bobby Smith for the first goal and headed the second one himself, and he was the man of the match when Tottenham became the first British club to win in Europe, beating Atletico Madrid 5–1 to win the European Cup-Winners' Cup. In that game, Dyson scored two goals and set up the other three. Nicholson was right, he was a little tiger, and I remind Nicholson every time we talk what a big favour I did letting him hold onto the midget. "He won you the Double," I tell Bill, "and you've got me to thank!"'

Having told his story, Bill Shankly swiftly asked me what I was doing with Revie.

'I'm up here working with the Leeds lads,' I answered. 'Leeds will win the Cup.'

'Arsenal won't be easy,' said Shankly, 'but that's a safe bet. Why don't you come to Liverpool and make my boys some money, and whatever you get for the Leeds lads, my boys are worth double.'

I promised Shankly I would come to Liverpool, and I was just about to put the phone down when he jumped in: 'Don't you ever forget that Tommy Smith is twice as hard as Hunter.' Then he added, 'Tell Nicholson I'll give him a ring if Tottenham win the UEFA Cup.' Shanks was laughing when he put the phone down.

I kept my promise to Shankly; I did go to Liverpool. I travelled up to convince the team to set up a players' pool at the beginning of the season and chip in all their off-the-pitch money: things like sponsorship, advertising, merchandising, public appearances, etc. After all, Liverpool won some silverware every season, so why wait until they were in the final before setting up a players' pool?

In the 1970–71 season, I had been involved in the Arsenal FA Cup final pool. Their official Wembley brochure, 'Inside the Gunners', contained action drawings I had completed of the Arsenal squad: players such as Frank McLintock, Bob Wilson, Pat Rice, Charlie George and George Graham. Everyone in the team was a household name and they all claimed their favourite breakfast cereal was Shredded Wheat. It served its purpose and helped pull a lucrative sponsorship deal. The Co-op and Esso were amongst those who took full-page ads. It was a big success, but I was aware that the six-week period between Arsenal winning their semi-final and playing in the final was much too short a time to roll out money-making ideas, get them marketed and still have a reasonable amount of time to sell them.

Lilywhite magazine, 1961

Ken Johnstone, the London-based agent and public relations executive, ran the Arsenal pool and although it was the biggest total ever achieved for a players' Cup final pool, when it was shared out amongst the squad of players, they were very disappointed. They picked up 'peanuts' compared to the huge financial jackpot they deserved and could easily have generated in a much longer time period. The many sponsors who could not get aboard – because time didn't allow it – missed out on a historic soccer milestone. Arsenal beat Bill Shankly's Liverpool in the Wembley final – Charlie George scoring the winning goal – and Bertie Mee's team completed the Double.

I travelled up to Anfield with a case bulging with potential Liverpool deals. It was back in the '50s that I'd started operating in the field of football merchandising and sponsorship, long before it became fashionable, and in those early days I persuaded Sweetule Products in Wood Green, North London, to put my drawings of international footballers on the back of their children's sweet-cigarette packets. Those packet-back cards today are valued at £7 for each card. At the same time, I went to the Master Vending Company in Cricklewood Lane, London, and sold them the idea of two football sets, each comprising 50 cards of my drawings of players, to be given away with the bubble-gum that popped out of their machines.

Deal followed deal. I knew what sold, but on the train travelling up to Liverpool in 1973 it was different. Liverpool sold themselves – everybody wanted a piece of them, especially when it came to Kevin Keegan. Every Liverpool deal in my bag stipulated that Keegan had to be involved. Having said that, Tommy Smith, the Liverpool – no, correction – football's Mr Hard Man, was equally in demand. Every deal in which the manufacturers needed to emphasise that their product was durable, tough and unbreakable was rubber-stamped with Tommy Smith's name. I believed when I opened my bag and threw the deals down on the table, I couldn't fail with the Liverpool players. I was even more convinced they would see the value of a players' pool set up at the beginning of a season, giving all that time and more to operate efficiently and effectively in selling the team. I was just as confident I would eventually get even Bill Shankly himself involved.

When I faced the Liverpool lads, I was immediately aware that Kevin

Keegan, who was sitting two rows back, was *the* big Liverpool star. He literally glowed 'Mr Endorsement'.

'As Liverpool players,' I said, 'all your off-the-pitch money – sponsorships, advertising, endorsements, manufacturing deals, public appearances, newspaper articles, photographs and any other money-making ideas – go into one big pot which we set up at the beginning of the season. All money you receive relating to your international careers is yours to keep.'

As I talked, I believed I was getting a very favourable reaction, but I was wrong. Keegan was obviously not impressed. He got annoyed. He got up. He walked out. Maybe he didn't like the sales pitch, or it could have been me, the cocky London lad, the 'pitcher'. Anyway, the Keegan exit meant the meeting was over. There was a lot of confusion. Some players remained seated, others got up and walked out, but not Tommy Smith. He immediately marched over in my direction. The light was behind Smith, but even his shadow when it hit me made me wince! Shankly was right: face to face he was the hardest man you could ever meet. I thought he was going to hang one on me – knock me cold.

'I agree with what you've been saying,' said Smith. 'You're right. No one player does it on his own. It's a team game; we're all in it together. It's one for all and all for one.'

I saw Tommy Smith a few weeks later when Liverpool came down to play Arsenal.

'I've spoken to Keegan,' said Smith. 'Why don't you come back to Liverpool and give it another go?'

'I'll give it some thought, Tommy,' I promised, but deep down I couldn't see it working. I never went back.

But this I will say: if Dyson was a little tiger, then Tommy Smith was the big cat – the maneater – the number-one hard man, and he didn't even have to tackle you to prove it.

CHAPTER EIGHT

Sir Alf Ramsey and Bill Nicholson: How Do They Compare?

As a player, I had the good fortune to play for the most part of my career under two footballing legends: Bill Nicholson and Sir Alf Ramsey. Looking back, it doesn't come any better than that. I was fortunate to see the two master football tacticians at work from a close-up position – two highly successful managers with, of course, a playing background at Spurs.

The similarities between Bill and Alf ran deep. Both won league championship medals with Spurs and both managed a team which did the same: Bill with Spurs and Alf with Ipswich Town. In that alone, they join the exclusive list of football legends who have achieved this remarkable Double. Dave Mackay won the title as a player at Tottenham and managed Derby County to the championship. George Graham won both as player and manager with Arsenal. Ted Drake did it playing with Arsenal and managing Chelsea. Howard Kendall won with Everton both as player and manager. Joe Mercer did it with both Everton and Arsenal as a player and with Manchester City as manager. Bob Paisley won both as player and manager with Liverpool and Kenny Dalglish did it with Liverpool as a player and both Liverpool and Blackburn Rovers as the boss.

I spent from 1964–1972 with Bill playing for Tottenham at White Hart Lane, and along the way Alf gave me 35 England caps, including one match as captain. Bill and Alf were both great bosses and in many ways were very similar to work under. This is not really surprising as they both played together in the all-conquering Spurs push-and-run team of the '50s. The discipline and the tactical know-how knocked into them during their playing days at White Hart Lane by their innovative manager, Arthur Rowe, survived the years and served both very well when they entered the manager's office.

I am often asked to compare these two giants of British football and to judge who I believed was the better manager. Well, I would never dream of putting one ahead of the other as, in their own unique way, they were both the absolute best. However, there were differences and I will highlight those differences and at the same time throw more light on just what made these two great managers tick.

Let's start with the most often asked question. Bill loved wingers, but Alf won the World Cup in 1966 with his 'wingless wonders': who had it right? The short answer to that one is that they both did. The truth is, Bill had three exceptional wingers at Tottenham – Jones, Medwin and Dyson – and football at the end of the day is all about players. Bill had the players – three great wingers to play in his Double-winning side of 1961. Alf wasn't so lucky, and he was forced into making a very tough decision in 1966. He could have played with wingers; he had Terry Paine, Ian Callaghan and John Connelly, who were good performers. They each played, but in only one game. Alf eventually decided against them and instead used his two full-backs, George Cohen and Ray Wilson, in a dual role.

It wasn't that Alf disliked wingers. He just knew that he didn't have a Stanley Matthews or a Cliff Jones in his squad, and so he had to plan his tactics accordingly. To Alf's everlasting credit, he got it right. It worked. England won the World Cup.

Players, not managers, dictate what system a team plays. A prime example of that was Nottingham Forest in their glory days under Brian Clough and Peter Taylor. They had the Scottish ball wizard John Robertson, who was what you would call a good line-winger. Stuart Pearce, or any full-back who played for Forest, would have been told to get the ball quickly to Robertson because Robertson, an exceptionally skilful ball player, could beat people, get down the line and knock in inch-perfect crosses. Cloughie had that ace in his bag and of course he was going to use his winger. He would have been crazy not to, and Robertson helped to win Cloughie trophies.

Alf was very clever and very tactically astute. He recognised he didn't have wingers with the world-class ability that would be required to lift the World Cup in 1966, so he played without them. Alf went with a flat back four – Cohen, Charlton, Moore, Wilson – with Nobby Stiles sitting just in front of the flat back four. This ensured that if anyone in the opposing side broke through the middle of the field, Nobby was there, ready to pick them up. Then you had the freedom of Alan Ball, Martin Peters and Bobby Charlton, with the fire-power of Hurst and Hunt, who were the two up front. That was the team – no wingers – and it worked for Alf for many years. Alf used his full-backs as wingers and the system worked so well he very nearly landed two World Cups.

I was fortunate enough to make Alf's side in Mexico in 1970 and I played the Nobby Stiles role in front of the flat back four when England set out to defend the trophy. I can give you a classic example of how England operated successfully with no recognised winger in the side. In the quarter-final game against West Germany, the ball was played to my feet 10 yards outside the penalty box in our half of the field. I looked up and, of course, there were no wingers to be seen. Fifty yards away, racing down the right touch-line, I spotted full-back Keith Newton. Immediately, I hit a long 50-yard pass to Newton who now, in possession, continued his run down field. He takes on the full-back, beats him, gets to the byline, crosses it and I hammer it home. Keith had become the winger. On the left, full-back Terry Cooper also performed the same dual role.

In 1966, full-backs George Cohen and Ray Wilson were, in effect, the English wingers, so at the end of the day Alf had his own version of wingers, although, of course, they were totally different to the style of wingers Bill played at Spurs. Alf's system during the 1966 World Cup had its dangers, the chief one being a situation where England lost possession and the full-back was caught upfield out of position, attacking the opposition's goal. To overcome this danger, Alf insisted that Nobby Stiles would come away from his midfield position in front of the flat back four when the full-back was attacking and move out towards the touch-line. In other words, Stiles had now taken up the full-back's position. Stiles had to cover on whatever side of the field the full-back had made his move upfield, and this meant a lot of running.

Getting back to how your players dictate how a team plays, another example came when I first went to Brighton as manager. I had two excellent wingers: Peter O'Sullivan on the left and Tony Towner on the right. O'Sullivan, or Sully, as he was known, could go past players, had a superb left foot and whipped in great crosses. Towner had plenty of pace, could go round people, get to the byline and put in a cross with his right foot. I had Peter Ward and Ian Mellor up front, and they both scored a hatful of goals thanks to those two superb wing-men.

O'Sullivan and Towner excited the Brighton fans, got them out of their seats, just as the likes of Jones, Dyson and Medwin did for Bill Nicholson. That's why Bill played with wingers. He had at Spurs three excellent players who could do the job. Wingers are exciting, yes, but you have to have the players with the skill and pace to excite. Bill had them and that suited him right down to the ground, because he put so much store on entertaining the fans. The best flying wingers consistently go past players and score goals, and nobody did it better for Spurs than Cliff Jones.

Unfortunately, Alf didn't have one in the Jones class and so his England team couldn't entertain in the same exciting way as Bill's 1961 Spurs Double-winning side. But, as I said, Alf made a brave choice in 1966. He had quality wingers available, but he wisely decided that, for England to win the World Cup, they needed to play without them. Alf devised a playing system which allowed him to do this. If he had had a Jones or a Matthews, he may have made a totally different decision. That is no criticism of the wingers that he had in the squad. They were class performers, excellent players in their own right, and Alf must have thought long and hard before he decided to back his judgement and play without them. No one can argue that he did not make the right decision.

Another question I am often asked is could Bill get as angry and as tough as Alf did in the infamous World Cup match against Argentina in 1966 when he stopped the England full-back George Cohen exchanging his shirt and he called the excessively physical South Americans 'animals'?

Well, yes, Bill could. I can remember a European game in Lyons when a French player kicked me full in the face and it finished up with the two of us getting sent off. Bill was so angry with the referee and the Olympique Lyonnais players that he burst into our dressing-room after the game in an absolute rage and stormed, 'When this lot come to our place, we'll absolutely murder them!'

I had never heard Bill say anything like this before and I had never seen him so angry with an opposing team. Eventually, Spurs were unlucky to go out on the away-goal rule.

As for work-rate, Bill and Alf held similar views. Bill expected his players to work hard, run and run, win the ball and score goals. Alf's expectations were no different. Indeed, I believe Alf's were even higher. He demanded more running, more chasing, for, at international level, it was much harder to win the ball back. A prime example of this was in the 1970 World Cup in Mexico when England played Brazil. It was midday and the temperature was 110°F in the shade. If you watch a video of that game, you'll see how hard, in that blazing heat, the England boys worked, how much running they did to get the ball off Brazil when they had possession, and they did it for 90 minutes.

Bill and Alf also acted in a very similar manner when they spoke to people. Both talked quietly in very short sentences and they kept it brief and to the point. When they had something to say, they never waffled on. But although Alf and Bill didn't say a lot, what they did say meant a lot. I well remember the morning during an England practice session when I was with Alan Ball and Martin Peters and we were trying to agree on the best method to take a free-kick awarded 10 or 15 yards outside the penalty box. Martin Peters wanted to take it the West Ham way, in which a player runs up and then runs over the ball and Peters steps in and bends the ball around the wall into the net – and, to be fair, Peters was excellent at accurately bending the ball. But I wanted to do it the Tottenham way, where a player runs up and then runs over the ball, I act as though there has been a change of plan, bend over as if to replace the ball, and instead chip it over the wall for the player who had originally run over the ball to collect and bang it into the net. But Alan Ball wanted to do it the Arsenal way. Again, a player runs up and over the ball and then . . . at that point, Alf walked over and interrupted.

'Gentlemen,' said Alf, 'we have Bobby Charlton, and nobody can hit the ball harder than Bobby. May I suggest we have a player who runs over the ball and then you, Alan, simply pass it to the side for Bobby to run on to and hammer into the net. Agreed?' And with that, Alf walked off.

During the match, we did get a free-kick awarded 15 yards outside the box. I stood there with Peters and Ball and we decided we would take the kick Alf's way – so Peters ran up and over the ball, I passed it to the side and Charlton hammered it. The ball literally whistled into the back of the net – one up for Alf, we all thought. In the dressing-room at half-time, Alf made his points on our first-half performance and then, with just a slight trace of a smile, added, 'I see the free-kick worked.' That's all he said. Alf was never one to crow and say 'I told you so'. And that was just one of the reasons we all liked him so much.

Another similarity between Bill and Alf was in the way they liked to be addressed by players. Both preferred, indeed insisted, that it was 'Bill' and 'Alf': none of this 'Boss' or 'Gaffer' which you hear a lot of today. I can remember the first time I reported for England duty in 1964. Alf came up to me and said, 'Welcome, Alan.'

I said, 'What do I call you: Boss?'

He said, 'NO. Call me Alf.'

The funny thing is that when I got my first job in management at Brighton in 1976, I wanted people to call me Boss. I didn't want any of this Alan stuff. I believe it was because, at the time, to show that I had authority, I needed that assurance behind me, something which spelt out 'hold on, I'm the Boss – I'm the one in charge of this club'.

Well, Bill and Alf didn't need that. They both had an unshakeable belief in their ability. They were able to go out and do things with an unbelievable air of authority which demanded respect, even when players called them by their first names. But I insisted people called me Boss at Brighton. I felt good about it. If someone had called me Alan, say a young ground-staff boy, I would have thought, 'Hold on, where is the respect coming from here?'

The amazing thing was that, although both liked to be called Bill and Alf by their players, it didn't help one little bit with conversation.

They were both very hard people to talk to. It was almost impossible to engage them in everyday chitchat; small talk wasn't a part of their make-up.

I can remember coming back with England from Scotland on a train with Alf after a game. There were a couple of football writers and several of the London-based players in our group and Alf just talked about the game – nothing else – just the game for about an hour. He then suddenly picked up the evening paper, grabbed a sandwich at the bar and that was the end of it: no chitchat, gossip or jokes; no discussion about the TV shows of the day or who he would favour at the next General Election. It was exactly the same with Bill: football was his life. He had little conversation outside the game. They were both like this: totally dedicated to football. Nothing else counted or mattered.

When the train pulled into the London station, we all got out and I remember my wife, June, was there to meet me. As we all stood on the platform, Alf smiled and shook our hands before issuing his well-rehearsed parting comment: 'Thank you very much, gentlemen. I'll be seeing you again, I hope. As long as you are selected!'

With that, he turned and walked away into the London night. Away, no doubt, to begin immediately planning for England's next match. It was, as I say, football, football, football with Alf and Bill, and their drive and intensity was all-consuming. It was almost frightening. But who can argue with the results?

Of the two, I believe Bill was the harder person to please. Alf would be very complimentary to players, although he would never let it show outside the dressing-room. Bill, on the other hand, rarely told his players they had done well, either inside or outside the dressing-room. As for the media in general, both tended to say as little as possible, or as little as they could get away with.

Alf's press conferences after England training sessions at Roehampton were unbelievable in their brevity. Blink and you missed them! In those days, only about 10 or 12 writers would attend and Alf would stride into the conference room and announce the team. Then he would say, 'Any questions, gentlemen?'

A journalist would immediately fire a question and Alf would fire back his answer in double-quick time and, in the same breath, announce to the journalists, 'Thank you very much. That's enough, gentlemen.'

At that, Alf would turn and walk out. It was over. Today, the England manager is committed to spending a great deal longer with the media answering endless questions in front of television cameras. It wouldn't have suited Alf or Bill, I can tell you.

Which of the two managers prepared you best for the upcoming match? Well, the answer to that is a dead-heat. Both Alf and Bill had the same trait: they were both very, very meticulous in the way they built up a team to the big day. Absolutely nothing was left to chance. Every angle, every possibility was covered and as a player you appreciated this. You went out onto the field determined to give your very best for Alf and Bill. You knew they had worked hard, and I emphasise that word *hard*. Now it was your turn.

Neither Bill nor Alf worried you too much with facts and figures about the opposition. Both worked on the same theory, that if each player won his individual battle with the opposing player, then the game would be won. Bill and Alf both drummed into us that if you didn't compete one against one, dominate your opposing player and become better than him, stronger than him, more determined than him, then you weren't going to win the match. Both Bill and Alf subscribed to that theory.

If you, as a player, didn't get that message and the worst happened – you didn't dominate your opposing player and the match was lost – what was the reaction? Well, here there was a big difference. Alf was much calmer in defeat, whereas Bill would, on occasions, lose his cool. He would really have a go at players. At times, I thought he was wrong to have a go at players individually, and as captain there were occasions when I stepped in to calm it down, but when Bill was having a more general go at us, he was usually absolutely right in what he said and the truth hurts – and it *did* hurt.

Looking back, I wish Bill had given out more 'well dones', because when, on the odd occasion, he did, you felt 10-ft tall and your confidence grew, and football, as we all know, is a game of confidence. Alf was better in this department, although he was by no means lavish in his praise. He would sit the team down and say, 'Thank you very much, gentlemen. I thought you played extremely well today.'

But Alf wouldn't say those sorts of compliments to us individually. He never picked out one player and said, 'Well done today.' He was always talking to the team. While Alf wouldn't pick out a player to praise, Bill wouldn't hesitate to pick out a player to criticise if things had gone badly.

It wasn't so much a player performing badly with Bill, it was more when they weren't doing what Bill believed they were capable of doing as a player. Bill's expectations were very high. He expected you to be brilliant, every week, and that was never going to happen.

Bill had worked with so many exceptional, skilful, gifted, international players who repeatedly turned on the magic over the years that it made his expectation of the players of my era impossibly high. He would work on the lines that if you had one of those days when everything went right and you played fast-flowing, skilful, exciting, attacking football and won, he would be looking for a repeat performance the following week. You had showed Bill what level you could reach, and if you didn't keep reaching that level then he wasn't a happy man and he showed it.

Alf was very different to Bill in the way he reacted to defeat. I suppose his biggest setback was losing to West Germany in the quarter-finals of the 1970 World Cup in Mexico. I was there; I played in that match and I scored one of England's goals and I can see Alf now sitting in the dressing-room and thanking the players for what they had done for their country. He was totally dejected, unbelievably quiet, and you could see that he was extremely hurt and upset inside.

We were all upset, I was upset, but I believe not one of us players was as deeply hurt as Alf, and I am sure that was because he always said that the 1970 squad was better than the 1966 one which did win the World Cup. There is not one single doubt in my mind that if the 1970 World Cup had been played in Europe, England would have retained the trophy. What beat us was the heat and humidity we faced in South America. It was totally alien to what we were used to.

Despite the bitter disappointment of that defeat, Alf stayed calm. He wasn't a cup-thrower in the dressing-room, but I have to say that Bill was on the odd occasion. I have no idea how Bill would have reacted to that defeat if he had been the England manager in 1970, but what I do know is that if one of his Tottenham teams had been 2–0 up and went on to lose 3–2 as we did, he wouldn't have been too happy about it. We may have heard the sound of broken china and a few other things smashed up against the dressing-room wall, but we will never know that one and, for all I know, Bill may have surprised us all and taken a more philosophical view.

Football has its sad moments and they are always very painful, as in Mexico in 1970, so a sense of humour can be a very useful tool for a manager. Alf definitely had one. He could have a laugh and a joke and at times could laugh at himself. I was never happier playing for England than when I saw Alf with a big smile on his face enjoying a joke with the players.

The funniest Alf moment I can recall was when he received his knighthood and became Sir Alf. We were playing down in Wales in the Home Internationals. As the players were leaving our hotel, Sir Alf happened just to be getting back from Buckingham Palace after receiving his honours.

'What do we have to call you now, Alf?' I shouted at him as he got out of the car.

Quick as a flash, he came back, 'Bastard – exactly the name you've always called me!'

With that, Alf got on the waiting coach with us and joined in as we all laughed our heads off. That was Alf – the other side of Alf.

I feel sure that Bill would have reacted in exactly the same way if he had got a knighthood, but, out of the two, I have to admit that Bill was the more dour character. There were very few times when Bill would join in a session with the players and have a good laugh, even when the atmosphere was light and we were all laughing and joking. It happened on the odd occasion, but not a lot.

Another area where Bill and Alf differed greatly was how they reacted to one of their players if he was sent off. If you were sent off for some reason that was stupid, Bill would give you the cold shoulder and look at you with complete disdain. He could, and did, make you feel very small indeed.

Contrast that to Alf, who would tend to take your side. He did this when I became the first player in an England shirt ever to be sent off in an England international match – the semi-final of the 1968 European Championships. We were playing Yugoslavia in Florence, Italy, in June and it was a brawling, rough house of a match. In the second half, I got caught by a vicious late tackle by Trivic, and I reacted instinctively with a kick. The referee pointed to the dressing-room and I was off for an early bath. Sadly, England went on to lose the match to a Dragan Dzajic goal.

In the dressing-room, I naturally feared the worst when Alf called me over to him, but I needn't have worried. He was so furious with the aggressive way the Yugoslavs had played that he simply said, 'Don't let it worry you, Alan. I think it was an injustice. I don't think anybody, if they were any sort of a man, could have stood for much more.'

He backed my actions 100 per cent, which, looking back, was questionable. I mean, when you turn round and lash out at somebody with a foot, you are expecting your manager to give you one hell of a rollicking. On top of that, this was a full England international match and the way the FA officiated in those days, they could easily have said, 'Right, Mullery, you'll never play for England again.'

But if the FA had adopted this stance and got nasty, I am sure Alf would have been in at their offices and would have told the FA Committee, 'Hold on, I want Alan Mullery. He's the one I want playing for me in the World Cup in 1970. I will continue to pick him.'

Alf would have backed me all the way, as he did with Nobby Stiles in a rather similar situation prior to the 1966 World Cup. This time, the England selectors actually came out and said, 'We don't want Nobby.' Alf stood his ground; Nobby played; England won the World Cup. Yes, Alf backed Nobby, and I can tell you it was an outrageous tackle by Nobby in an international match that caused all the arguments.

To be honest, I was very surprised that Alf backed me like he did in 1968. I knew I had done wrong. I never, in all my career as a footballer, came across another manager who would stand by and back his players as much as Alf did. The $64,000 question now is, would Bill have backed me like Alf did in Florence in 1968?

Well, I think you've probably worked out the answer to that one – I have to say I don't think he would have. He would have gone the opposite way to Alf and, bless him, would have given me the tremendous rollicking I probably deserved! Certainly, if Bill thought I had done wrong, he would not have sympathised.

However, having said that, I must state that there is a big difference in managing club players and international players. I don't think Bill would have ripped into England players like he did at club level if he had been manager of England. At international level, you are dealing with players who have proved they are the best in their position: players who have passed through the mill at all levels of the game and have shown the commitment, skill, discipline and self-belief that is required to represent their country. A manager has to take all that on board and I am sure Bill would have done just that and tempered his criticism accordingly.

Alf was, as I say, very laid back with the England players, but I wouldn't be surprised if he had laid into his Ipswich Town players when he won the Third Division title, the Second Division title and then the First Division championship to bring the Suffolk club unbelievable success.

Despite getting away with the sending off in Alf's book, I certainly didn't get let off by the public. Even to this day, I am still often referred to as the first England player to be sent off when I am introduced at a function – and that despite a career of 35 England caps, an MBE and a captain's role at Fulham and Spurs. That one kick in Florence in 1968 was costly.

Let's end by listing five areas where Bill and Alf were very much the same: they were both outstanding coaches; both had the same attitude to referees – don't argue with them, they never change their minds; both liked to have half-backs as their captains; both trusted players and treated them as men; and finally, neither got over-excited if they won a big game.

But the biggest thing they had in common was that they were both dedicated football men – different in some ways, but both exactly the same when you measure them up against greatness. They were both legends whose names will live on as long as football is played. I am lucky and very grateful to have played for them both.

* * *

My co-author Paul Trevillion was lucky enough to actually watch Bill Nicholson and Alf Ramsey play in the great Spurs side of the '50s, and here he remembers some highly successful wing-play tactics that involved both Bill and Alf:

Alan Mullery was absolutely right to point out that when Ramsey dispensed with wingers and won England the World Cup in 1966 with his 'wingless wonders', he did not have a dislike for wingers. In fact, in the famous Arthur Rowe push-and-run team, Ramsey developed a very simple and very effective tactical move that involved the Spurs goalkeeper Ted Ditchburn and Sonny Walters, the wing-man at outside-right.

It was Ramsey's coolness and ability to play beautifully judged, accurate passes that made the move work so successfully. Every time Ramsey was on the ball in possession in the Spurs penalty area, both Ditchburn and Walters were on the alert, ready if Ramsey decided to put the move into operation.

When the opposing left-winger was close to Ramsey, the move was on, and Ramsey usually – not always, but usually – went ahead and pushed a back-pass to Ditchburn. Ramsey would then run into an open space to receive a throw from the Spurs goalkeeper, by which time Walters would have stolen in and moved behind the opposing defenders. The skill factor in the movement was the pace and accuracy of the Ramsey back-pass. The ball had to be hit slowly enough for the opposing outside-left to be tempted into sprinting forward in an attempt to beat Ditchburn in the race to the ball. But always, Ramsey put sufficient hidden pace into the back-pass for Ditchburn to be favourite and collect. It was always very tight, very close, but always very successful.

Ditchburn would then throw the ball to Ramsey, who immediately hit a long pass to Walters, who was already on the move, and the flying wing-man scored a lot of goals from this simple ploy. When Tottenham won the First Division championship in 1951, Walters scored 15 goals, and he always attributed half of those to the Ramsey back-pass tactic.

Said Ramsey at the time, 'It was a simple little tactical move. I hit the back-pass back to Ditchburn just hard enough for the opposing outside-left to think he could get it – so when Ditchburn threw the ball to me he was out of the game. There was one less opponent between me and our winger, Sonny Walters, which made it easier for me to make a pass and for Walters to collect it. Walters scored a lot of goals from that move.'

Lilywhite magazine, 1954

Lilywhite magazine, 1953

Bill Nicholson presents a study in concentration as he completes a high follow-through with perfect balance in the push-and-run days of the 1950s.
(© EMPICS/Alpha)

'Turf' Cigarettes: a series of 50 footballers produced in 1948. Each card is valued at £2 in 2005, which is more than the original price of the full packet of cigarettes.

Newspaper cutting of the Tottenham Hotspur Football team 1946–47
published in January 1947. Back row (L–R): G. Hardy (late trainer), G.
Ludford, A. Willis, E. Ditchburn, V. Buckingham, R. Burgess, S. Tickridge.
Front row (L–R): C. Whitchurch, L. Bennett, G. Foreman, J. Hulme
(manager), L. Stevens, L. Medley, W. Nicholson.
The newspaper cutting has been signed by W. Nicholson, the first signature
Trevillion collected. Some of the other signatures in Trevillion's autograph
book are of these famous Spurs players.

ABOVE: Trevillion stands in the spot where he collected his autographs, which has now been renamed 'Bill Nicholson Way'.
RIGHT: 1 October 1960: Tottenham Hotspur beat Wolverhampton Wanderers 4–0 and completed the record of 11 games won at the start of a season. Published in the *Tottenham Weekly Herald*.

Maurice Norman signs an FA Cup-final programme before Tottenham's 2–0 defeat of Leicester City to complete the Double. There is no sign of a shaky hand! Norman, like the rest of the Spurs lads, was in control, ready to make history.

Nicholson and Blanchflower discuss team tactics at the Cheshunt
training ground in Hertfordshire, a few days before Tottenham
completed the Double at Wembley. (© PA/EMPICS)

The Tottenham Hotspur 1960–61 Trevillion cartoon of all the players who that season went on to achieve the Double is complete with all their signatures underneath. Published in the *Tottenham Weekly Herald*.

Spurs celebrate with the FA Cup after their 2–0 win against Leicester City which secured the Double (L-R): R. Henry, B. Brown, P. Baker, C. Jones, D. Blanchflower, T. Dyson, L. Allen, B. Smith, M. Norman.
(© EMPICS/Alpha)

Tottenham Weekly Herald cartoon: the 1961–62 season. Spurs retained the FA Cup, beating Burnley 3–1.

The 1962 European Cup-Winners' Cup. 'Super Spurs' beat Glasgow Rangers 5–2 and won the away leg 3–2. They went on to destroy Atletico Madrid 5–1 in the final.

Team and *Lilywhite* magazine wish Dave Mackay 'Good Luck'. Tottenham beat Chelsea 2–1 in the 1967 FA Cup final.

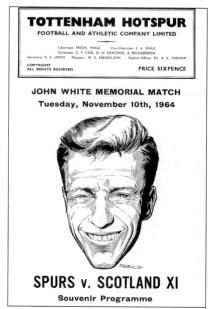

The John White Memorial Match programme: the day when all football wept.

Tottenham's goal-scorer Martin Chivers, Bill Nicholson and captain
Alan Mullery hold aloft the League Cup after their 2–0 win
over Aston Villa in 1971. (© EMPICS/Alpha)

1972: Tottenham beat Wolverhampton Wanderers in the UEFA Cup final.
Spurs captain Alan Mullery holds the Cup as he is carried shoulder high
by teammates Mike England and Pat Jennings. Also in the picture:
Ralph Coates, Alan Gilzean, Martin Peters, Joe Kinnear, Cyril Knowles
and Martin Chivers. (© EMPICS/Alpha)

Bill Nicholson and Paul Trevillion share a joke and some Tottenham memories in their last meeting at the Tottenham Hotspur football ground.

Tottenham Hotspur display case in the Bruce Castle Museum containing just some of Trevillion's drawings and football memorabilia. It also contains the Bill Nicholson League Cup final 1973 tracksuit top. Tottenham beat Norwich City 1–0 in the final.

Nicholson also liked to set up his wing-man for a raid on goal, as Freddie Cox, who patrolled the Spurs right-wing before Walters made the position his own, explained.

'Bill Nicholson was excellent in the air,' said Cox. 'He could really get up there. That's why he could play at centre-half. In that position, he was a match for the likes of Tommy Lawton and there's never been anybody better in the air than Lawton. Bill didn't just head the ball away, he got up there over the ball and directed it to safety, which always meant towards the wing. I had an understanding with Bill. He knew I was always ready for one of his headed clearances. They often set me up for a run at goal, and many a time I scored. I was always happy Bill was in the team because he never neglected his wing-man.'

In the 1951 championship-trophy-winning season, Ramsey did set Walters up for a lot of his goals, but Bill, with his ability in the air, also added to Walters's goal total.

CHAPTER NINE

Bill's Love of Hard-working Wingers

An intriguing side of Bill Nicholson's management style was his love of wingers. There is no doubt that his greatest ever side, the 1961 Double-winning team, owed a huge amount to three superb wing-men – Cliff Jones, Terry Dyson and Terry Medwin – who, apart from delivering inch-perfect crosses for the likes of Bobby Smith and Les Allen, also knew how to defend. This was an essential ingredient in the ideal Nicholson winger.

The fact that Nicholson never put together a second Double-winning side, or even a championship-winning side, was, in my opinion, down in no small way to his failure to find wingers in the Jones–Dyson–Medwin class. Bill searched and searched and, although he used high-class wing-men such as Jimmy Robertson, he was never able to draw together that magic 1961 wing formula which powered Spurs to so much glory.

Let's take a closer look at just what Bill expected his wingers to do and why he found Jones, Dyson and Medwin so hard to replace. If you look back to Bill's early days as a manager, he seemed to have a blueprint for wingers. The winger had to be a dribbling winger and he had to be quick. He had to be able to help the full-back in a defensive duty so he had a job to do when Tottenham didn't have the ball. On top of all that, Bill wanted wingers to score goals as well.

If a winger was attacking down his respective left or right side, Bill would expect the opposite winger to be in the box with the centre-forward and the inside-forward, so that there were three people who could be hit by the ball from either side of the field.

Terry Medwin was a highly talented performer with a little Stanley Matthews-like jink, whereby he would jink inside, push the ball past the full-back and off he would go. On top of that, he was a lovely crosser of the ball and could also hit the target from 25 yards. He was a beautiful striker of the ball.

Jones had fantastic pace. He could go at people and beat them with ease. He would drop his shoulder and be away. He was predominantly a right-footed player, which almost sounds silly for a player who played, in the main, on the left side.

In full flight, Cliff was one of the quickest players of his era. If a defender touched him, he was up in the air and it was a free-kick for Spurs. As a goal-scorer, he was as brave as they come. Many times, I saw a Spurs player cross the ball from the right and Cliff would get in a diving header, and often a defender trying to clear the ball would accidentally kick Cliff in the face. Cliff would walk away with blood pouring from a cut somewhere above the eye, and he'd be too delighted about heading the ball into the back of the net to care.

Jones was literally the perfect winger and Bill was a very lucky man to have him. My admiration for Jones is such that I would compare him favourably with possibly the most famous winger of all time, the late Sir Stanley Matthews – and Stanley was one of my heroes as I grew up. Cliff could do everything Sir Stanley could do – and more.

One of Sir Stanley's great tricks on the right wing was to go straight up and attack a full-back, shape to go to the left, drop the shoulder, push the ball down the line past the defender, race on to it and then cross a great ball.

If you think back to the 1953 FA Cup final, it was Matthews who made three of the goals and they said it was his Cup final, and yet Stan Mortensen scored a hat-trick. I can't name another game in which a player who scores three goals is not named 'Man of the Match'! But it was the wing-wizardry of Sir Stanley that captured the imagination of the public, and it will always be known as 'the Matthews final'.

As I said, Jones could do all that Sir Stanley did – but even more because of his goal-scoring ability from wide positions. If you wanted the mould for the perfect winger, look no further than Jones. He gave Bill great service over the years, not only in the Double-winning side of 1961, but also in the years after.

In 1964, when John White was tragically killed by lightning on the golf course, I remember there was a lot of talk in the papers that Bill was going to buy Johnny Haynes from Fulham to fill that hole, which I believe would have been perfect, but Haynes said, 'No. I want to stay at Craven Cottage.'

Bill decided to switch Cliff from being a wide player, where he was as good, if not better, than anyone in the country, to an inside-forward position, but Cliff was never the passer that White was, so it was not a success. Another problem was that every time Cliff got the ball, he naturally wanted to run with it instead of passing from an inside-forward position.

As for Terry Medwin, he again had a very quick, lively pace. He had a bigger build than Cliff, but again was a great striker of the ball and a good crosser.

In Jones and Medwin, Bill had two great wingers, but he wanted more. Bill would insist that, once they had lost possession, they had to get back behind the ball into the positions where they could help the full-backs. Bill would always emphasise that it was you against the other fellow, so it was one-against-one. In my position, it meant that the opposing midfield player was the one I had to dominate.

Jones and Medwin had to dominate the full-backs in the opposing team. Bill insisted on this. Bill had a set pattern of play which involved the full-backs and the wingers. He was very hot on this. Let's take an example. In the Double side, the moment the left-back, Ron Henry, got the ball, the first pass he would look for would be to Jones wide on the left. On the other side, the right-back, Peter Baker, had to make sure the first person he got the ball to was Medwin. If he couldn't get Medwin, he would go for Blanchflower in the middle of the field and, likewise, Henry would aim for Mackay in the middle. Bill's orders were always that the full-back had to look first for the winger and play the ball off quickly in order to give him time to get into a position to take the opposing full-backs on.

It was a very straightforward plan and it worked. It was so simple – when the full-back got the ball, he would look wide and hit the winger, and off they would go on one of their penetrating runs, looking to attack the full-backs. If the way was blocked, they would simply pass the ball back to Henry or Baker and they would try another route: either a short pass to a midfield player or, on occasions, a longer one up to Les Allen or Bobby Smith.

Bill would stress this time and again to his full-backs, that the first person you had to look for was your winger, because if you didn't feed him he could be standing out wide for ages without receiving the ball – out of the game – and that, in Bill's mind, was a crime. When you had wingers of the quality of Jones, Medwin and Dyson, you had to use them.

The fans always saw Jones as their flying winger who would go on those spectacular mazy runs into the opposition's half, but Bill would insist that Cliff also fulfilled his other role: that of ball-winner and defender. The fans did not see that side, but I can assure you we players did. If Cliff didn't fulfil his dual role, then Bill would come down on him like a ton of bricks.

Bill expected his wide men to be helping out when they didn't have the ball. He demanded that his wingers be up and down that field, doing long runs, long sprints, always on the go, up and down the line. Bill, it must be said, was very demanding on his wingers. If a winger wasn't defending properly, Bill hated it. He knew full well that the opposition weren't going to give you the ball back – you had to fight to get it – so Bill expected all his wingers to do their jobs properly, and that meant working hard and doing a tremendous amount of running when the opposition had the ball.

Another side of Cliff Jones which was often ignored was his total commitment. I saw him literally fighting to win the ball with brilliant sliding tackles, head-on clashes, pure physical determination. This wasn't the spectacular side of Cliff's game, but it was equally important. Without the ball, he couldn't have gone on those fabulous mazy runs.

I often spoke to Ron Henry about Bill's wingers and he told me that, in his opinion, Terry Dyson was an even harder worker than Jones. Although Terry never had the electric pace of Jones, he could run all day, he had a great drop of the shoulder and he could go past full-backs and score goals.

Cartoonist Paul Trevillion's impression of Cliff Jones, rapidly returning to form after breaking his leg.

Tottenham Weekly Herald,
1958

This work ethic Bill had in regard to his players makes for some interesting thoughts concerning more recent superstars. For example, in my own personal opinion, and I don't know if it would be Bill's, David Beckham would not be the sort of player that Bill would have had in his Spurs side. I am not for one moment suggesting that Beckham is a lazy player, but what I am saying is that nearly all of David's work is done from deep positions, long cross balls. You never see David go past a player in the same way that Jones, Medwin or Dyson could and did. I know the modern-day game has changed compared to what it was in the '60s, but Bill's emphasis was that you must have wingers that beat full-backs because, if you have that, it pulls opposing defenders out of position.

A good way to judge just how good a winger is is to get the views of a full-back. George Cohen, whom I played with at Fulham and who went on to win a World Cup winner's medal with England in 1966, always said: 'Cliff Jones was the most difficult person I ever had to mark.'

Cohen found it so tough partly because he was a very quick and powerful full-back and when Jones, on one of his runs, took George on, all George had to do was touch Cliff and he would go flying through the air, getting Spurs a free-kick. I know George didn't like playing against Jones at all, and yet George could handle most people.

Bill always built his sides around good wingers, and that goes a long way to explaining why the teams which followed the Double-winning side never quite had the same magical success. The fact is that Bill found it almost impossible to replace Jones, Medwin and Dyson at their best. Who wouldn't? These were completely exceptional players for a manager, and the wingers that followed should in no way feel they let Bill down – they didn't: it was simply that they had three hard acts to follow.

Let's take a look at some of the wingers Bill brought in following the end of the 'Big Three'. The first was Jimmy Robertson, who came from Scotland and was easily the quickest player at the club. Then there was Jimmy Neighbour, who came through the ranks. Then Jimmy Pearce had a spell on the wing, as did Frank Saul. But Bill's problem in those days was he never had a natural outside-left. By 1967, Jones was, in Bill's opinion, past his peak and, as I've mentioned before, Bill was ruthless with players once they were heading downwards. The upshot of it was that Jones ended up at Fulham, where he had two excellent seasons. He could still go past people and George Cohen was pleased because he didn't have to mark him any more!

Immediately after the 1967 Cup final, Bill went out and bought Roger Morgan from Queen's Park Rangers. Roger was a very skilful player. He had lovely control, could beat people, and he could score goals too. Unfortunately, though, he never really made it at Tottenham. There were great expectations, because he had shown he had outstanding ability at QPR, but for one reason or another it never really happened for him. My own feeling was that he suffered because he was following a world-class winger. The expectation among management and fans was that if you brought in a winger, he had to be like Cliff Jones, but the truth was he was nothing like Cliff Jones.

Morgan was a different type of player to Cliff, but because he played wide on the left-hand side, the crowd expected him to be a direct swap. As a result, the supporters began to get on his back, which was a shame. Roger was a nice lad to have around – very funny with a great sense of humour.

I suffered with the crowd too, in a similar way to Roger, when I first arrived at Tottenham. They tended to think that because I had been brought in to replace Danny Blanchflower, I would be just like Danny. I wasn't. I was Alan Mullery. The fans thought I should be a carbon copy of Danny, but I wasn't. It was never going to happen that way – Danny and I were different types of players.

Bill found these situations difficult to handle. He was a crowd-pleaser at heart and his attitude would be, 'If the crowd are getting on your back, well, they are getting on your back for some good reason.' He would always sympathise with the crowd, because clearly if they weren't seeing what they expected to see, they were being let down.

The fact was, if you didn't play well and, more importantly, entertain the crowd, Bill wasn't happy. Basically, Bill's attitude was, 'Look, if the crowd are giving you stick then you aren't doing your job.' He was very tough about it and you had to get on with it and handle it the best way you could. It was a major problem for Morgan, and my feeling is that he never found a way around it.

Looking back to those days, it is easy with hindsight to see that Bill made a big mistake with the signing of Morgan. Before the event, I would have been of the same opinion as Bill and I would have gone for Morgan as well, but, as I say, in hindsight it was a bad move which didn't work.

Bill was also guilty, I believe, of making another rare error when, for some reason or another, he and Jimmy Robertson had a falling-out and Bill decided to let Jimmy go to Arsenal. In that deal, he took a player in exchange and that was David Jenkins, a winger. Now Jenkins was a very honest, charming man, but he never had anything like the pace of Jimmy Robertson and poor David took some horrendous stick from the crowd – he was never given a chance. There is no doubt that around this time Bill was into a very tricky situation. He had tried to replace Jones,

Dyson, Medwin and Robertson with Roger Morgan and David Jenkins – two wingers who, although they worked very hard, did not quite fit the bill. It was never going to be easy for Nicholson to fill those holes, but I am sure he couldn't have imagined just how hard it was proving to be.

This is in no way a criticism of Bill. He tried everything he knew, including spending a lot of money, to solve his problems. I know; I was at the club at the time and I saw the countless hours Bill and Eddie Baily spent checking out wide players – the search was endless. It's also no criticism of the wingers Bill used during that time. They all did their very best and more. It was simply that, through no fault of their own, they weren't the owners of the God-given talents gifted to the likes of Jones, Dyson, Medwin and Robertson.

* * *

Such was the impact that Bill Nicholson's Double team made on football that it wasn't just Spurs fans who were in raptures. My co-author, Paul Trevillion, has found that rival players too were huge fans – none more so than the Manchester City legend Mike Summerbee. Here, the exciting flying City wing-man recalls those days in the early '60s:

Mike Summerbee on Bill Nicholson

'It was the 1960–61 season. I was a young lad of 17 playing for Swindon in the Third Division, and Bill Nicholson's Tottenham team, which was breaking record after record, had everyone in football asking the all-important question: could Spurs do the Double?' Manchester City legend Mike Summerbee remembered.

'In those days, to win both the league and Cup just wasn't on. The last club to do the Double was Aston Villa, way back in 1897. I wanted Tottenham to do it. That Spurs side Bill Nicholson had built, with players like Mackay, Blanchflower, White and Jones, played fast, attacking football that was out of this world. They were unstoppable. They scored over 100 goals, won the league, beat Leicester in the final and achieved the impossible – the Double. I was pleased. Just about everybody in football was pleased, because Tottenham had done it in great style.

'Today, winning the Double is almost commonplace, and so it should be. There's only half a dozen teams with a realistic chance of winning anything, so there's not the fierce, week-in week-out competition there was in Nicholson's day. When he achieved the Double, it was very different. Nearly every team – Arsenal, Manchester United, Everton, Manchester City, Chelsea, go right through the league – had great players; they could on their day play teams off the park. Every match was a battle.

'The pitches were terrible. You could be ankle deep in mud one week and playing on concrete the next. You had to get to Wembley to play on grass! Not like the bowling greens they have for pitches today. There were no polyester shirts to allow the rain to run off. It was cotton, and when it rained, you played in an overcoat! Today, there's no tackling, no goal-mouth scrambles. In Nicholson's Double year, the tackles went flying in. The refs allowed it. It was hard; it was physical. You sat in the bath after a game and counted your bruises, and the ball – well, let's just say a nine year old could kick today's match ball half the length of a field. It was a different game then and that's why I rate the Nicholson Double team so highly. You had to be some player to perform, and players like Blanchflower, Mackay, Haynes, Law, Charlton, Best, Greaves, Moore – the list is endless – turned it on every week. It makes me laugh out loud when people say to me, "Could those players do it today?" That's not the question. The question is: "Could today's Premiership superstars have performed way back in the '60s?" I have to wonder. But, this I do know: put the likes of Law, Best, Greaves, Mackay on today's bowling greens with the referee's protection, and watch them go. They would have you standing up out of your seat for the entire game.

'When I was playing for Swindon and I heard that Bill Nicholson was showing a keen interest in me, I couldn't sleep for a week. But in those days a player didn't get a lot of say when he was transferred. Joe Mercer swooped in and I was a Manchester City player. I was one of the first pieces of the jigsaw that the Joe Mercer–Malcolm Allison partnership put together, in what was to be a magical period in the history of Manchester City. I was very lucky to be part of it.

'Nicholson at Tottenham was both coach and manager, and he let his team do all the talking. It was different at City. The Mercer–Allison duo were back-page headlines every week. Allison was much more than just a great coach. He was an unbelievable talker, a master in the psychological preparation of teams and players and, with his flamboyant nature, he was a walking, talking side show on the touch-line during a match.'

Summerbee then made a point: 'I believe when Malcolm Allison was at Sporting Lisbon, he must have consciously or subconsciously made a big impression on the very young José Mourinho. I believe – I might be wrong – that the charismatic Chelsea manager, Mourinho, has modelled himself on Allison and, let's be fair, Allison was the ultimate in self-expression.'

Summerbee laughed, 'The Mercer–Allison team which won the Cup and European Cup-Winners' Cup was a lot different to the Chelsea side Mourinho fields. Everyone in the City team that won the silverware was an Englishman. What a game it would have been if that City side could have played the Spurs Double team.

'The massive squads full of internationals at the top Premiership clubs mean players are not forced to play every game and still they talk of tiredness. The time to be tired is when you're 38 and finished. Then you're forced to sit out, and watching is *no* substitute for playing.

'When the Nicholson Tottenham team did the Double, they used just 17 players and that was about it when the City players were winning their medals.'

I was very impressed with how much Summerbee remembered about Bill Nicholson's Double team, so I jumped in with the Spurs 'catch' question. 'Mike,' I said, 'how many of the Spurs players who played in the Double team do you remember?'

Without hesitation, Summerbee fired back: 'Brown, Baker, Henry, Blanchflower, Norman, Mackay, Jones, White, Smith, Allen, Dyson.'

'Mike,' I said in amazement. 'Everybody puts Greaves in the Double team, but you remembered it was Les Allen.'

Summerbee had his answer. 'Those people who put Greaves in that Double team never saw them play. How can you *forget* Allen? He scored nearly 30 goals and never missed a match.'

As always, Summerbee was right. Allen slammed home 27 league and Cup goals and he did play in every game.

'There are occasions when I meet up with Mackay,' went on Summerbee, 'and it's a privilege to be able to talk to him about football, and Bill Nicholson and the Double team always crop up. You can't talk to him about Tottenham without mentioning Nicholson. He *was* Tottenham and *is* Tottenham and he will *always* be Tottenham.

'I met Nicholson many times,' continued Summerbee. 'It was always a pat on the back and a "well done" when I was a player. When I finished with the game, I never missed an opportunity when I went down to Tottenham to watch City play to talk to him. Nicholson always found time and the thing that impressed me most was the way he treated everybody with so much respect, no matter who they were.

'The last time I visited Tottenham,' recalled Summerbee, 'Martin Peters and big Martin Chivers took me into the luxurious Tottenham hospitality suite. I looked everywhere for Nicholson. "He's in another suite in another part of the stadium," they told me. I couldn't believe it. I shouldn't have had to look for Nicholson. He should have been there in his own place of honour so we could all get a glimpse of the great man and, if we were lucky, a chance to talk to him. I missed out that afternoon and that rates as one of my saddest memories in all my years in football.'

CHAPTER TEN

Management:
the Nicholson–Mullery Way

There is no argument that Bill Nicholson was the absolute master of his trade when he ruled the roost at White Hart Lane during his trophy-winning glory years as manager. How Bill would have coped today is a matter of some speculation. The plain fact is that the manager's role now is almost unrecognisable from the job Bill did so successfully and so gloriously in the '60s.

In those days, Bill had complete and total control over everybody at the football club and would just report to the board of directors. He would simply turn up at the board meeting and give his own personal report of everything that was happening at the club. Bill had a personal secretary and there was a club secretary and that was it.

Today, a manager's prime concern is the players in his squad – buying new ones and selling players is no longer required. In Bill's day, not only did he do that, but he had a say in every single aspect of the running of the club. Today, most of the non-player business would be done by a chief executive. Bill had none of that back-up, and it is not in the least surprising that he was busy with the Tottenham business affairs seven days a week. A manager in those days managed the lot. Everything that happened at Tottenham came from Bill's 'yes' or 'no'.

Today, you have a chief executive who deals with contracts and you have agents wheeling and dealing on behalf of their players. In Bill's day, agents, in the main, just didn't exist. If a Tottenham player wanted a wage rise, he didn't send his agent in to see the chief executive, as happens now. No, the player would go and see Bill and I can tell you for a fact that if Bill had been subjected to some of the wage demands made by today's players, he would have got up and physically picked up the player and thrown him out of his office.

Bill's negotiations were very simple. He would make you an offer, and if you didn't accept it, he would turn to you and say, 'Fine, you stay on the wages you're on now.'

I remember in my first year at Spurs in 1964, I was on £70 per week, and before the start of the following season, I got an official letter from the Tottenham club informing me that they had given me a £10 per week rise! On the first day back at pre-season training, I knocked on Bill's office door and his familiar voice bellowed out, 'Come in.'

I poked my head round the door and said, 'Oh, Bill, by the way, thanks very much for the wage rise.'

Bill looked straight at me and said, 'Now, Alan, don't start thinking you're a good player because I've given you some extra money.'

That was Bill's way. There was no hint or even a suggestion of 'you deserved it, Alan'.

Today, all those wage problems are dealt with by a chief executive and an agent, so the manager has one less problem. But poor Bill and the other managers of that era did the lot. Today's management world is literally a million miles away from what it was in the '60s and early '70s.

When I got my first job in management at Brighton in 1976, I never discussed anything with agents, because I had noticed that Bill always refused to deal with them. I went down the same road. I had no time for them. But now, of course, I can see that a manager is forced to deal with agents, because of the unbelievably big money that has entered the game.

Back in Bill's days at Tottenham, players basically had little say in the transfer process; it was just sorted out between the two clubs concerned. A player's agent never – well, not to my knowledge – entered the scene. Mind you, there was the murky side, with rumours of bungs and money in brown envelopes changing hands at motorway eating houses. But in Bill's case I can genuinely say that his name was never featured in such talk, and rightly so, because Bill was whiter than white – completely honest – a true gentleman of the game.

Whilst certain aspects of the management business today are totally different to 40 years ago, there are still some that are almost identical. Take the meticulous preparation that some managers go in for today. Well, that hasn't changed one little bit. I guarantee that Bill Nicholson was just as meticulous with his planning as José Mourinho is today.

Bill's meticulous build-up to a match would even extend to what a player would eat. If a player ate a certain meal on a certain day and had a good game, then Bill would insist he stick to that meal for the next match. He would often come up to me after I'd had a good game and ask what I'd eaten beforehand. He would write that all down and the idea would be to repeat the diet which had led to the good match I had played. Some players performed better on a big steak, others on an omelette, others on rice pudding, while some even just preferred cornflakes!

When I went into management at Brighton and Hove Albion, I took quite a lot of Bill's careful planning and attention to detail with me. For example, locally there were at least six golf clubs and I got in touch with each of those clubs and told the secretary and then the golf professional that, after Tuesday, could they please make sure no Albion footballer played golf. Having got the message over, I then made absolutely sure that it was being followed.

Another rule I had was that players couldn't go out after Wednesday night. Of course, some players did, but I always found out and I would fine them wages. The money went to the charity Guide Dogs for the Blind. Indeed, I believe the Albion players put more guide dogs on the streets of Sussex than any other donor back in those days!

Naturally, when I went to Brighton in 1976, I was heavily influenced by all I had learnt from playing under Bill at Spurs. I remembered how annoyed Bill would be if his players didn't play as well as he believed they were capable of and I knew how hot he was on players giving the crowd value for money.

I can remember a game at Brighton's Goldstone ground being played on a bitterly cold day in atrocious conditions, with rain and snow coming down. In the first half, Albion's performance was so poor it looked like they were playing a practice match. Now, on that day, we must have had 28,000 fans standing freezing on the terraces in the rain and snow, having paid good money to do so.

I was absolutely fuming. I stormed into our dressing-room and gave them all one heck of a rollicking for two minutes, then I threw them back out onto the pitch. Normally when it was wet and snowy, the players were allowed to change their shirts and shorts. I wouldn't let them do it. I made them keep their cold, soaking wet gear on and go out of the dressing-room and stand in the rain and snow in the centre circle out on the pitch.

Then I made my way up to the director's box and took my seat to enjoy the scene and listen to the crowd who were all muttering, wondering what on earth was going on. As I say, 28,000 were standing, freezing on the cold, open terraces, getting soaked to the skin, so my players got a good feeling of just what it was like.

All I can say is that it had the desired effect. Believe it or not, after just 25 minutes, we had hammered in seven goals! I knew my Albion team were a good side and in that first half they were not playing to a level I knew they were capable of. As I say, that sort of thing would send Bill mad and now, as a manager myself, I could see why. The crowd, too, knew that the team could do better and that they were being short-changed. In the second half, they were fully entertained and went home to their hot cup of tea totally and completely satisfied.

As a manager, you are always looking for the perfect player: the man with all the qualities to inspire the team and rule supreme. Bill, I would say, during my time at Spurs, only had one: Dave Mackay. He truly had all the qualities a manager looks for. The nearest to a Dave Mackay I had at Brighton was my skipper, Brian Horton. He was multi-talented, but lacked Mackay's ability to score goals on a regular basis. I was a huge admirer of Horton and he was most certainly an extremely important part of Brighton's success at that time, which saw them reach the old First Division – the equivalent of today's Premiership.

At that time, I would have picked Horton as the most likely of the Albion players to have a career in management after his playing days were over. Like Mackay at Tottenham, he had great leadership qualities and these qualities did indeed, as they did for Mackay at Derby, serve him very well in management.

Although I was always trying to follow the Nicholson blueprint as a manager, I must admit that on one or two fronts our styles were totally different. Bill's man-management approach was entirely different to mine. Bill, as I have said, rarely gave out praise to his players. I was the opposite: I was always praising players. I would put my arm round a player and say 'well done'. I would give players credit for what they did. However, like Bill, I was always ready to give out a rollicking if I felt a player wasn't doing his best. My attitude was that if a player performed to his ability and did the business, I would hand out lavish praise. If he didn't, then I was upset and I let him know it. On these occasions, I was like Bill. When he was angry, he would start throwing things around the dressing-room. As a Tottenham player, you had to learn to duck and, I have to admit, I would do the same thing if I felt the players had not performed and let the team down.

When I first went to Brighton, I would phone Bill quite often to get his advice on how to handle certain players and also if I had a problem that I couldn't solve. I was looking for words of wisdom and Bill never once let me down. Bill would always stress to me that I had to always show who was the boss. He would stress that, in any conflict with a player, no matter what, I had to end up being the winner.

The classic example here involved one of the Spurs fans' favourites, Joe Kinnear, who had been signed from Tottenham by Peter Taylor, my predecessor at the Goldstone. When I arrived at the South Coast club, I could see a problem arising, even on my first day. Joe Kinnear was a senior player and I could see at once that he, along with three other players, had a lot of influence on several of the younger boys in the squad. In other words, there was the potential for a head-on clash. It was Joe or me.

I rang Nicholson and explained the situation. He was adamant. 'Alan,' he said, 'you've got to show who the boss is.'

It was very awkward. I classed Joe as a good friend, but I could see problems ahead if I didn't immediately stamp my authority on the situation. At the time, my own feeling was that Joe was too heavy and I told him he was well overweight and had to lose some of it. Joe wouldn't have it. He insisted he wasn't overweight. This was an immediate challenge to my authority, so I sensed Joe was going to be a big problem. Acting on Nicholson's advice, I was determined that this was the battle I had to win. If I hadn't won that battle with Joe, I probably would not have been the success I was at Brighton.

I owe Bill a big thank you on that one. When I talked to Bill, he made it very clear what I had to do and emphasised I had to act quickly. He said to me, 'Look, Alan, you may have played with Kinnear at Spurs, but now it's a different situation. You have got to make a choice. Do you let the player win – or do you win?'

I found the decision I had to make very tough, and I gave it a huge amount of thought, because, as I say, Joe was a good pal of mine. We had enjoyed plenty of laughs when we were together at Tottenham. I liked the fellow and this made it all the harder, but Bill was right. I stood my ground and it did come down to a head-on clash. Joe insisted he wasn't overweight and said, 'Pay me up my contract, Alan, and I'm off.'

I shook my head and said, 'No, Joe. I'll play you in the reserves and I'll have you in training every day and I'll personally work on your weight problem myself.'

Anyway, in the end, the club agreed to pay Joe a certain amount of money, which he accepted, and the battle was over. Joe left and the way was clear for me to stamp my influence on the squad.

It wasn't pleasant and I was far from happy about it. I wished it could have worked out differently with Joe, but, as Bill told me, it was a battle I had to win if I wanted to be a successful manager.

That first season, the Brighton boys went on to win promotion and the ride to the top division of English football had begun. It was my first managerial confrontation, but over the years Nicholson had faced many similar situations at White Hart Lane and, each time, Bill would have faced up to the issue; he wouldn't have ducked it. If a battle was to be fought between player and manager, then Nicholson was always up for it, and you can bet on it, he always won the battles during his reign at Tottenham. Indeed, it was those individual victories that allowed Bill to cast his magical influence over many Spurs teams. It allowed Bill to do it his way. Nicholson's achievements at Tottenham are in the record books for all to see.

The fact that I had this very good relationship with Bill when I set out on my managerial career does, of course, beg the question: could such a partnership have worked if I had got the Spurs job in 1974 when Nicholson quit? Well, I have to admit now, I did apply for Nicholson's job when it became available, but as we all know it went in the end to Terry Neill. If I had got the Tottenham manager's job, I can tell you that I would not have let Bill leave the club. I would have made him chief scout immediately: a post he did eventually return to do.

Indeed, I would have kept, in the main, the Tottenham staff who were already there, for the simple reason that they knew the club inside-out. Terry Neill came in, and, for reasons I can well understand, made three or four changes to the backroom staff, and those sorts of decisions can sometimes just make the difference between success and failure. It's a thin dividing line, as all managers know.

The fact is, for Terry Neill, with his very strong Arsenal background, it was always going to be an uphill struggle at Tottenham. In hindsight, his appointment does appear to have been a big mistake. It would have been just as strange if it had been the other way round and someone had gone from Tottenham to Arsenal as their new manager. The Tottenham directors did have plenty of options at the time that Nicholson quit and my own feeling – and, as I say, with hindsight it is all a lot easier – is that Eddie Baily may well have been the man to have taken Tottenham on to further glory.

I know the Tottenham directors may have been a bit worried about Baily's outspokenness, but surely if you are a director, you should never fear the manager? If a director thinks a person is the right man for the manager's job, even if he can be outrageous at times, then he should take him. Look at José Mourinho: a person who can certainly be outrageous, but who has been a great success at Chelsea.

Yes, Baily was outrageous at times, I agree, but my strong hunch is that he may have been the man to carry Tottenham to more trophies. Baily knew the players; he knew how to handle them. He was a great coach and tactician and, above all, he knew how the club operated.

As for myself, if I had got the Tottenham job, I would have adopted most of Nicholson's managerial dos and don'ts, including allowing my captain to be the manager on the pitch. Having said that, I would have differed slightly in the handling of players' families. To Bill, wives and families were very much secondary to football. If a player had family problems of any sort, Bill just wouldn't get involved. In my time as a manager, I have to say I took the opposite view and would go out of my way to encourage players' families to feel part of the football club. I would even go as far as sending flowers for a family birthday. I made a point to always remember things like that. Something like sending flowers to a player's family would never have even entered Bill's head.

Another area in which I differed from Nicholson on the management front was in media relations. I loved talking to the media and giving them quotes on the club and players. If I had a player who wasn't performing as he should, I never hesitated in airing my views to the press. Bill would never do that. But I believe it never harmed a player and, more often than not, it made him even more determined to prove me wrong. Nicholson was very much an introvert with the press. At times, Bill deliberately avoided journalists. He wouldn't want to be interviewed in case he said the wrong thing, or even the right thing and was misquoted. If a press man wanted him to talk technically about football, then he was fine, but if the questions were about how a certain player performed or didn't perform, then Bill wasn't interested; the interview was over.

Nicholson and I did see eye to eye on fitness and the vital role it played in football at the highest level. Indeed, some Tottenham players who were close to Bill held the belief that Nicholson's 1961 Double-winning side scored very heavily on the fitness front, to such an extent that fitness could well have been the key ingredient which gave Spurs the vital edge over so many teams during that history-making season. I certainly took Nicholson's obsession with fitness into my management career, and at Brighton I established a rigorous pre-season training regime which served the club well during my years on the South Coast.

I would get the players running up very steep hills, and when I first arrived at the club, I would join them. After two or three seasons, though, I had put on a bit of weight, so I stood back and let the players do it on their own. We would do long-distance work over golf courses and I would get good local distance-runners to come in and take the boys on. As it did for Bill, it paid off for me.

Over the years, people have asked me how Nicholson managed to maintain a very strong team spirit in all his sides, especially as, more often than not, his teams would be packed with 11 international players who were all highly talented individuals. The answer, I believe, has to be that as soon as he saw that a player was restless and possibly hankering after a transfer, he would rarely try to persuade that player to stay at the club. He didn't want an unhappy player and would rather him leave than stay and spread unrest. Also, it has to be remembered that, in the '60s and '70s, all the top players were earning much the same money, so there was no jealousy on that front. It certainly helped a great deal as regards team spirit.

Bill could be pretty tough and unemotional in dealing with players who expressed a desire to leave. I remember that, the season after I had scored the winning goal in the 1972 UEFA Cup final, I went to Nicholson and said, 'Bill, I think it's time I moved on.'

'Fine,' said Nicholson. 'Come into my office; here's six clubs you can talk to.'

Nicholson didn't turn round and say, 'Don't be daft, Alan. You're my captain – you're my leader – we are in Europe!' That wasn't Nicholson's way.

Above all, Nicholson's style of management was based on total honesty and he was always just that with me. You knew exactly where you stood with Nicholson. Indeed, Bill often said, 'The first quality a manager needs is honesty. A dishonest manager will never last very long, because his players will find him out and lose their respect for him. Respect is the single most important factor in a player–manager relationship.'

I also know from my many talks with Bill that he felt it was important that a manager had played, coached or worked at the top level at football clubs, and the more success he had achieved, the better. Players can be ruthless, and they will find any chink in the manager's armour and exploit it, especially when results are going badly.

Certainly, it helps if you can bang down a few international caps on the table and say 'here are my credentials'. I was fortunate enough to be able to do that at Brighton and at other clubs that I managed, and it soon ended arguments.

Then there was Bill's work ethic. He was a manager who believed in putting in the hours, first on the training ground and then in the office. Come the evening, Bill would get in his car and attend games, so he was virtually on the case almost around the clock, seven days a week. That was the Nicholson style, but it didn't suit everyone.

As for myself, I have to say that, although I worked extremely hard, I could never reach the unobtainable heights of devotion that Nicholson achieved. It just wasn't my way of doing things when I was a manager. We are all human and we are all different.

The ability to motivate a player is another key aspect of management and Bill had his own methods in this area, although, compared to, say, Bill Shankly or Brian Clough, they were definitely very low key. Bill would come into the dressing-room 60 minutes or so before kick-off and would quietly go round and talk to each player on a one-to-one basis, rather than address the whole team with a rallying call. Bill would go through each player's duties and would carefully list the strengths and weaknesses of a player's opposite number.

As I say, Nicholson's style was very different in tone to Clough or Shankly, but in its own way it worked every bit as well. I always believed that one of Bill's greatest strengths as a manager was his photographic memory. He could recall every incident in a match, however small. That was vital: especially at half-time, when Bill had just ten minutes to remember every incident and make tactical and constructive comments. I was always impressed by Bill's analysis of every little detail of the game being played; he missed nothing. Because of this remarkable photographic memory of Bill's, you knew that when you were out on the park, you could get away with nothing. Bill would have seen it and would remember it even better than you.

Funnily enough, Sir Alf Ramsey, too, had a marvellous memory when it came to analysing a game. Having played most of my football under Bill and Alf, you can say that all of my mistakes were remembered quite clearly – I got away with absolutely nothing!

Another area of management that is vital to success is the manager's relationship with the chairman. If that is unsatisfactory, it often leads to failure on the pitch. In this area, Nicholson was fortunate because the chairmen he worked under – Fred Bearman, Fred Wale and Sidney Wale – all, without exception, allowed Bill to run things his own way. I would go so far as to say that this was a key reason for the Nicholson 'glory, glory' years at Spurs. Bill was allowed total freedom to get on and do things his way, and that is crucial if you want to be successful as a manager.

I was lucky in that area at Brighton, where, during our highly successful years as we rose to the old First Division, I managed to develop a great working relationship with chairman Mike Bamber and the directors. At the end of the day, this relationship played a very important role in Brighton's success.

Humour is another aspect of good management, and while that could never be described as one of Nicholson's strengths – although it must be said that he did enjoy a good laugh – he was always aware of its importance. Maybe it was luck or was it Nicholson being wise, but at Tottenham he surrounded himself with a host of characters who could literally make you shake with laughter. The likes of Eddie Baily, Danny Blanchflower, Joe Kinnear and Jimmy Greaves, to name just a few, could always be relied upon to keep a very happy dressing-room.

Strangely enough, the end of the Bill Nicholson management years at Tottenham were brought about by one of his greatest strengths – namely, Bill's capacity to work endless hours every day. When Nicholson resigned in 1974, there were many wild rumours flying around as to why he made that decision, but the simple truth was, and Bill fully admitted it to me, he had burnt himself out – he needed a rest.

Having witnessed his frightening workload and the accompanying hours he put in, I was not in the least surprised it all ended with burn-out. Certainly, in my time at Tottenham, I never saw Nicholson take what I would call a proper holiday, and I gather that that was the case during his entire reign as boss. Nobody was to blame; this was entirely Bill's choice, his way of doing his job, and it finally caught up with him. But my guess is that if Nicholson had the opportunity to do it all over again at Tottenham, he would do things exactly the same.

I never knew or even saw Nicholson delegate jobs at the club, and that sort of pressure upon one man is enormous. I believe he recognised that his method of management worked so successfully there was no need to change it.

When Nicholson quit, I had already moved on, but it must have shocked and upset the players at Tottenham. I know they all wanted him to change his mind, and a visit by Martin Peters and Pat Jennings very nearly persuaded Bill to do just that. I wasn't totally surprised myself, as I had bumped into Nicholson just a few months before he had decided to call it a day and, reading between the lines, I got the firm impression that things at Tottenham were starting to weigh heavy and were beginning to get him down.

Although burn-out was the prime reason, I do know that the ugly rise of football hooliganism didn't sit well with Nicholson. After all, here was a man who loved stylish football, and violent hooliganism was at the very opposite end of the scales. I can understand his deep loathing of it. Subsequent events on that front proved Nicholson to be absolutely correct, as we all know only too well; football hooliganism was to grow and very nearly killed the game we all love.

Nicholson had left Spurs, but, after recharging his batteries, he couldn't resist further involvement with the game he loved and he had a spell helping Ron Greenwood at West Ham. By then, Keith Burkinshaw had replaced Terry Neill as boss at Tottenham, and Burkinshaw brought Nicholson back to White Hart Lane to act as a consultant. In 1991, Nicholson finally retired and became club president.

It was a total privilege to have known and worked with the man. He guided me into a totally new world of football excellence and dedication. Bill Nicholson was up there with Busby, Shankly, Stein, Ramsey: all the greats. I was a lucky man to play for him and learn from him.

Let's recall what some of football's top people told the *News of the World* when the great man died in October 2004, aged 85.

> Bill always wanted us to go forward and play football. If we were winning 5–1, he would rather us draw 5–5 than think negatively. He was a perfect gentleman. I've already cried today.
>
> Dave Mackay

> I was asked recently if the Arsenal team of 2004 was the best I had ever seen. I said no. Spurs in 1961 were even better. They were so fluid and exciting.
>
> Terry Venables

> He was an unbelievable manager: an unbelievable man. The team Bill put together in 1960–61 raised the bar. He stood for total football and nothing less.
>
> Pat Jennings

He did so much for the game and for the Tottenham club. He drilled into us that the most important thing was the club and its fans, and I would put Bill alongside greats like Shankly, Busby, Clough and Ferguson.

Cliff Jones

I'd put Bill alongside any manager you can name, and that's from Bill Shankly to Brian Clough.

Martin Peters

Bill was one of the greatest blokes, if not the greatest, that I've ever worked for. He firmly believed we should be paying for playing for Spurs.

Jimmy Greaves

The main reason I signed for Spurs was the honest approach of Bill.

Steve Perryman

He was not only one of our great football managers, but also one of our great coaches: solid, honest and totally reliable.

Sir Bobby Robson

Nicholson was 'Mr Tottenham', the cornerstone of this great club.

Glenn Hoddle

He was respected not just for what he achieved, but also for the way he achieved it.

Gary Mabbutt

I had 12 great years as a Tottenham player under Bill Nicholson and could not have wished to have played for a better manager.

Joe Kinnear

In November 2004, I joined many of Tottenham's greatest players for a special Bill Nicholson memorial service at White Hart Lane. It was a

very moving and dignified occasion. All of Bill's family attended, along with 8,000 Spurs fans.

The very high regard that Bill was held in was evident in the turn-out. The likes of Greaves, Jones, Peters, Hoddle, Mabbutt, Harmer, Chivers, Kinnear, Beal, Coates, Saul, Jennings, Robertson, Clemence, Perryman, Pratt, Shreeves, Pleat, Keane, Defoe and Carrick were all to be seen. The atmosphere was electric, yet, as I say, dignified.

Six players came forward to speak: Greaves, Jones, Chivers, Perryman, Hoddle and Mabbutt. They all spoke with great, genuine, heartfelt affection for the legend and the man that was Bill Nicholson.

Meanwhile, films were shown on the big screen at White Hart Lane capturing memorable highlights of the Nicholson years. It was a day I shall never, ever forget, and the climax said it all. Nicholson's daughter, Linda, stepped forward and thanked everyone and made a very special mention of the supporters: 'We know Dad loved you every bit as much as you loved him,' she said.

A final prayer and blessing followed and then 85 white doves were released in honour of each year of Bill's life. Off they flew, out of the ground. Glory, glory hallelujah.

* * *

Renowned football coach John Cartwright held similar views to Bill Nicholson on how the game should be played, and here he tells my co-author, Paul Trevillion, about their shared football beliefs:

John Cartwright on Bill Nicholson

'It was a bright morning, not too cold, and the sun was shining as I started my football coaching session,' remembers John Cartwright. 'Almost immediately, I became aware that I had an audience. It was only an audience of one, but the lone person watching I recognised at once. It was the unmistakable figure of the Tottenham manager, Bill Nicholson, who was standing on the far side of the field. I carried on with the coaching session. I became so involved, I forgot about the presence of Nicholson. That was, until I glanced across in his direction.

He had gone. Obviously, my first reaction was Nicholson was not too impressed, but I was wrong. I spotted Nicholson again; he had moved to a more comfortable vantage point and he was sitting on a small grass slope.

'Nicholson stayed there as I continued to put my coaching theories into practice. I believe football is a sideways game; you should always play on the half-turn in both attacking and defensive situations. When I finished, I walked over to Nicholson.

'"Well, what did you think, Bill?" I asked.

'Nicholson smiled, glanced at his watch and replied, "I'm still here."

'I checked my watch. Nicholson had been watching for over an hour – proof enough, I thought, that he had been impressed.'

Cartwright, who had been a player with West Ham and Crystal Palace, went on: 'I had met Nicholson on several occasions over the years at football awards and functions during my time as FA Youth Coach for Under-18s, coach at Arsenal, technical director at the National Football School at Lilleshall and PFA technical director and youth coach at Crystal Palace.

'I always enjoyed talking football with Nicholson; we shared the same ideals. We believed the game had to be played skilfully, fairly and be as entertaining as possible. But the prevailing climate in the game made it very difficult to play football in this way. With so much at stake, it is almost an accepted practice to cynically foul a player who, with a bit of individualistic skill, takes the ball past you. Take your eyes off the football field and you can relate this to everyday life. When two people with an extensive vocabulary argue, it will end at worst with nothing more than a raised voice. But if two people argue – one with an extensive vocabulary; the other with no gift for words – the chances are it will end with a raised fist. It's the same in football. When the skilled player encounters the less gifted player, it usually ends with a raised boot: an open admission by an inferior player that he cannot match another player's skill. The great ball players have the strength of character to learn to live with this rough treatment; they are never intimidated by the raised boot.

'Nicholson, in common with every top coach, agreed that even the greatest players can lack something – but that something is never courage.

'The qualities Nicholson looked for in a player were strength of character, self-belief and skill. Nicholson searched these players out and signed them: Blanchflower, Mackay, Jones, White, Greaves, Smith, Gilzean, Peters and Mullery, etc. – talented, skilful players, full of creative ability, who excited, entertained and won silverware.

'I believe England today is sadly lacking in players with artistic ability. There is too much emphasis on the physical side of the game and not enough on the basic skills. The better technical qualities you have, the more tactical options are available to you.

'I still have the Nicholson dream. I strongly believe this country can produce the footballers with the necessary skill to play fast, skilful, exciting football that entertains and wins in style. At Premier Skills in Worcestershire, we have a coaching course that preaches the following "commandments":

Football: The Twelve Commandments

Thou shalt have perfect touch when controlling or passing the ball.

Thou shalt be confident and cool-headed playing in tight situations.

Thou shalt run with the ball in a positive manner at every opportunity.

Thou shalt have the skill and self-belief to dribble past opponents when necessary and with effect.

Thou shalt confidently keep possession when no attacking advantage is available in all areas of the field.

Thou shalt be prepared to battle to earn the right to play.

Thou shalt strive always to get into a position to make a decisive contribution.

Thou shalt have the courage to attack the ball in a crowded six-yard box when the boots are flying.

Thou shalt overload situations – get numerical supremacy – whenever possible, with or without the ball.

Thou shalt courageously mix the game-style in both attacking and defensive situations.

Thou shalt combine cleverly and imaginatively with colleagues.

Thou shalt finish positively and accurately from all distances and from all angles.

'These are the stepping stones for the next generation of Blanchflower, Mackay, Greaves, White, Jones, etc, who I believe could bring back the Bill Nicholson glory years at Tottenham Hotspur.'

* * *

The late Sir Stanley Matthews recalled when he met Trevillion in the United States prior to the 1994 World Cup how the true character of Nicholson the player shone out like a beacon in the heat of battle:

Stanley Matthews on Bill Nicholson

I was sipping a cup of very hot coffee while Sir Stanley Matthews was drinking from a glass filled with spring water.

'You drink too much coffee. It's not good for you,' said Matthews, who was looking at the drawing of himself which I'd told him had been published in the *Weekly Sporting Review* in 1953: the year he'd won his FA Cup winner's medal. Matthews had signed it right across his face at the time, and now he was studying his signature.

'It hasn't changed over the years,' observed Matthews with a smile. 'You could read it then and you can now. It certainly doesn't seem like I signed that drawing 40 years ago.'

It was 1993. I was in America sitting at a table with Stan Matthews in the Umbro hospitality lounge. Stan Matthews, Gordon Banks, the Brazilian Rivelino and I had been invited by Umbro to join the 'Soccer Blast USA Legends of Soccer Tour'. It was one of the many American soccer promotions to publicise the 1994 World Cup.

'I still can't believe it's 40 years,' repeated Matthews. 'An FA Cup winner's medal – every player dreams of winning one of those. I am one of the lucky ones, and you need a bit of luck or a bit of good fortune to win one.'

'Can you still remember the two FA Cup semi-finals you played against Tottenham?' I asked Matthews.

'Do I remember them? I'll say I do! They stand out more than the finals I played in. Everything hangs on the game. You can actually feel the tension, the pressure, in a semi-final. You have to win to get to

The Maestro himself... the one and only STANLEY MATTHEWS (who has autographed this drawing by artist TREV)

Weekly Sporting Review & Showbusiness, 1953

Wembley. And those two semi-finals Blackpool played against Tottenham are as clear in my mind today as the day I played in them.'

Matthews sat back in his chair. He had put down his glass and was now helping himself to a salad sandwich. I decided to pass on the hamburger and fries and join him.

'Funnily enough, luck played no small part in those two semi-final games against Tottenham,' recalled Matthews. 'Blackpool could easily have lost both of them – but we didn't, and I'll tell you why.'

Matthews was a slow eater but a fast talker. He raced on: 'The '48 semi-final played at Villa Park had Tottenham leading 1–0 with just four minutes to go. Len Duquemin had got their goal. Tottenham, who were then a Second Division side, had troubled us, and with just four minutes to go it looked as if it was going to be good enough to take them to Wembley. In an effort to upset the Tottenham defence, I had moved infield, and with the clock rapidly ticking down I collected a pass. I was just over the halfway line, in the Tottenham half of the field. The Spurs captain, Ronnie Burgess, ran towards me. I decided to take him on and go for goal. Then, out of the corner of my eye, I spotted Stan Mortensen. I could also see in front of me Tottenham's Nicholson and Ludford, or it might have been Buckingham, but there were two of them, so I knocked the ball forward between the two Tottenham defenders for Mortensen – who could really move – to run on to and race between them. Like a flash, Mortensen was on the ball. He went straight between them, but the two Tottenham defenders turned and raced alongside. Nicholson was favourite to make the tackle. I had seen those tackles a hundred times when Mortensen was in full flight. Even the best defenders could not get in a fair tackle: Mortensen moved too quickly. It was always a foot in and Mortensen would go crashing to the ground and it would be a free-kick. I waited for Nicholson to tackle as Mortensen, moving at top speed, approached the penalty area. I was sure Nicholson would tackle. He had to tackle and Mortensen had to go down, but Nicholson kept running alongside, forcing Mortensen wide of goal. A couple of times, Nicholson moved to tackle, but he held off, and Mortensen was now well wide of the near post. The Tottenham goalkeeper, Ted Ditchburn, moved out to further narrow the shooting angle. I thought Nicholson had done his job and the goal chance had gone, then Mortensen shot and Ditchburn dived. He got his fingertips to the ball, but it travelled on, hit the inside of the far post and went in. We were level.

'I mentally thanked Nicholson. He had played Mortensen fairly, but had come off second best. It was extra-time.'

Matthews leaned forward in his chair: 'Tottenham's quick-passing game had run us off our feet, but Tottenham had run themselves into the ground, and Mortensen's goal, so late in the game, had knocked the heart out of them. Mortensen scored two more goals in extra-time to complete his hat-trick and put Blackpool in the final.'

Matthews was now picking from the fruit-salad bowl. 'The 1953 semi-final against Tottenham, again at Villa Park, was every bit as dramatic,' recalled Matthews. 'Blackpool were up against the Tottenham push-and-run side. I think only Les Medley was missing from the team that had won the Second Division title and First Division title in successive seasons. Most of the Tottenham players were in the beaten '48 side. They were determined not to slip up this time. Even so, Blackpool scored first.

I floated across a corner, Bill Perry climbed above everybody and headed the ball, which flew into the Tottenham net.

'Tottenham then, with their quick, accurate, passing game took over, but we stood firm and held out. Then, early in the second half, Tottenham's Eddie Baily – what a great player he was – completely wrong-footed the Blackpool defence by stepping over the ball, which ran to the unmarked Len Duquemin, who hammered it past George Farm into the net. Tottenham, with their quick-passing game, were now running the show. They looked the likely winners and there was a very good reason for this. The Aston Villa officials had decided on the morning of the match to water the pitch, but they left it too late. The water had not soaked in and it created a very slippery and very fast skiddy surface that favoured Tottenham's game of quick passing along the ground.'

Matthews leaned even further forward in his chair: 'With seconds to go, we hit a long ball out of our defence towards Bill Perry on the Blackpool left wing. Tottenham's Alf Ramsey was quick to spot the danger. He was across and first to the ball. Perry was still racing in and so too was little Jackie Mudie, but the ice-cool Ramsey had the ball at his feet. The whistle was about to blow. All Ramsey had to do was play safe, kick the ball into the crowd, and it was time. But that was not the Ramsey way. He decided to keep the ball in play and to pass it back to Ditchburn in the Tottenham goal. It could have been the slippery pitch, which was now playing tricks – in odd areas, it had dried out; it might have been a bad bobble; it could have been any number of things; but Ramsey didn't hit the intended pass back strongly enough. It held up for Mudie to nip in and Ditchburn was beaten, the ball was in the back of the net and, thanks to Ramsey, Blackpool were back at Wembley and this time it was a winner's medal.'

Matthews got up, did a little stretch, then sat down again.

'Have you ever talked to Ramsey or Nicholson about those games?' I asked Matthews.

'Yes,' came back the instant reply. 'I asked Ramsey if now, on reflection, he wished he had kicked the ball into the crowd. Ramsey gave me his usual half-smile and shook his head.'

'"No – never. You can only play football one way. You "pass" the ball to a teammate."'

'There was no answer to that. Ramsey, in playing his football in the true spirit of the game, gave me my opportunity to collect the "holy grail" – an FA Cup winner's medal.'

Matthews got up, stretched again, but this time he did not sit down.

'Let's walk,' said Matthews. I followed. 'Nicholson said pretty much the same when I talked to him,' said Matthews, as I lengthened my stride. He was a brisk walker.

'I must admit, I thought Nicholson might have had second thoughts about the '48 semi-final. I said to him, "Bill, looking back to the semi in '48, do you now think you should have brought Mortensen down and given away a free-kick?"

'Nicholson butted in. "Stan," he said, "if I had deliberately fouled Mortensen and chopped him down and Tottenham had gone on to win the Cup, I would not have been able to go up and collect my medal."

'That summed up Nicholson. He wanted a gold medal with the inscription "FA Cup Winner", not "Cheat"!

'Neither Ramsey nor Nicholson collected an FA Cup winner's medal, but they didn't miss out,' laughed Matthews. 'In fact, as managers, the two of them did very well. They set new standards with their teams, playing attractive, winning football with the same high level of sportsmanship. Ramsey won the big one: an England World Cup winner's medal. Nicholson won three FA Cup winner's medals, plus a few others. When I look back, I've got those two great sportsmen to thank for two Wembley finals and my gold winner's medal.'

As I left Matthews to continue his brisk walk – it was almost a trot, around the vast Baltimore Arena – I remembered Ramsey and Nicholson when Tottenham won the 1951 League Championship saying this was the proudest day in their football lives. I wished at that moment I had the *Tottenham Hotspur Football Club 1951–52 Official Handbook*. I would have given it to Matthews; he would have understood. It had, inside the front cover, a picture of the championship team, 1950–51. Both Ramsey and Nicholson, standing side by side, are in it, and alongside are the words:

> For when the One Great Scorer comes
> To write against your name,
> He marks – not that you won or lost –
> But how you played the game.

CHAPTER ELEVEN

No Room for Sentiment

A savage stinging pain ripped through my stomach muscles and stopped me in full flight as I tried to race back towards our penalty box to get in a tackle on the Stoke player who had just gone past Phil Beal. Nicholson acted at once: I was pulled off. He could see I couldn't run, and, as I walked towards the touch-line, I feared the worst.

I noticed the first sign of the problem during the games I played at the end of the 1970–71 season. It was a sharp, stabbing stomach pain. It had been a long, tough season. We had played plenty of games in winning the Football League Cup and finishing third in the league and I had been pushing myself really hard, literally busting a gut. I thought a good rest would put it right. It meant missing the England matches during the summer, but I had no choice. I needed to rest up and allow my body to repair itself.

Before the start of the 1971–72 season, Nicholson hammered out his expectations loud and clear. Tottenham had to win everything. But of the three cups up for grabs, I believed if Bill could win just the one, it would have to be the UEFA Cup. Success in Europe Nicholson valued above everything else.

The summer rest had done me good. I felt completely fit and refreshed and I was confident that Tottenham, with the players we had, could repeat our success of last season and win some silverware. But the season was only a few games old when I felt again the first painful twinges in my stomach muscles. I decided to keep the injury to myself, but, with each game I played, it got progressively worse. It began to severely affect my running, turning, twisting and even my kicking. I couldn't even pass a ball without pain.

I was not playing to the level I expected of myself. I imagined Nicholson must have been of the same opinion. It was time to tell him. Bill listened; he had heard it all before. He said it was a stomach strain. He emphasised that Dave Mackay had had the same problem and played through the pain barrier. He'd got over it. Bill stressed it was up to me to do the same and to do it playing at my best.

It was nothing more than I expected of Bill. As always, he had been fair. He had accepted I had an injury, and he was still prepared to keep me in the team. But he had made his point clear: I had to run the injury off and play my part in helping Tottenham win matches.

I tried playing in an elasticated corset, which, to a degree, helped keep my stomach muscles in place, but it wasn't the complete answer. Football is a physically demanding game. There's a lot of stretching to be first to the ball, to turn a bad pass into a good one, and even with the corset I was finding it increasingly painful and difficult to do those things and to be on top of my game.

Nicholson remained patient and I was grateful for his support. He was giving me every chance to play through the pain barrier – to run it off. He honestly believed that like Mackay I would get over it. It was down to me.

There was no way during a game I could nurse the injury. Playing in midfield meant I was always in the action and my game was based on full commitment. I had never held back and even now I never looked for an opportunity to do so, so there was no hiding place. I accepted I would have to play in pain, but the injury showed no sign it would fade away and with each match I was having to accept it looked pretty hopeless. The game against Stoke signalled the end and the medical diagnosis was 'strained pelvic muscles'.

I was told it would take weeks to heal and it meant I had to rest and go to Tottenham to receive deep heat and electrical treatment twice a day. The thought of being out of football for several weeks was a massive blow. I was very depressed. It was the Tottenham fixture list which gave me a much-needed boost. Tottenham were at home against Everton, so I decided to go along to watch and meet up with my England teammate Alan Ball, who I liked a lot. Ball had read about my injury and he told me he had just recently got over the same problem.

Ball told me it had taken six weeks before he was playing again. We talked about the injury and we compared notes on every movement – running, kicking, twisting, turning – that produced the stabbing pain. It turned out that the pains were brought on by exactly the same movements as Ball's. His injury matched mine and he was back playing in six weeks. I felt a lot better.

I was even happier when, a few weeks later, Ball left Everton and went to Arsenal for a record fee and Ron Suart, who was the manager at Blackpool when he had Ball as a young lad, answered the critics who had written him off when Ball played with the injury. Suart believed that Ball was playing better than ever and he said in the *Sunday People* that, 'It's nonsense to compare Ball with a car engine that's been run flat out for six years and is burnt out. It's the opposite. Ball's been run in. Ball's still world class.'

It was great to know that this injury left no permanent damage. But, unlike the time after my car accident when Bill insisted I played against Manchester United even though I was strapped up and virtually on crutches, he did not, as the weeks of treatment passed, show any signs of urgency in getting me back to playing in the first team.

Tottenham were doing very well without me. They were getting some great results, but I believed a fully fit Alan Mullery was still worth his place in the team and although I'd had the one setback, trying to return too soon, I was now rapidly approaching full fitness. I was back playing, if only for the reserves. The weeks passed and it was quite obvious that Nicholson was happy to let things carry on as they were. I did not share that view. My place was back in the first team.

I had played four hard games, plenty of running and tackling, in the reserves, with no ill effect. I believed the injury was well and truly behind me. I was back to full fitness; I was ready for action.

I now had to prove myself in the first team, but still Nicholson had not shown any signs he was in a hurry to put me back in the side, so I had to act; I had to see Nicholson. I realised – even though I was still the Spurs captain and had played close on 400 first-team games, scoring nearly 30 goals and collecting 35 England caps – it was not going to count with Bill when we talked. That was history, and Bill was no historian. It was all about how you were playing now – today. What you had done in the past was for your scrapbook, not Bill's. Every player who was in the Tottenham first team was there on merit and was treated as an equal. Bill had no favourites. It didn't matter who you were or how many caps you had. Nobody got special treatment. He was fair and honest with everyone, but only his opinion, and his alone, decided how well you were playing. If you were in the first team and you were playing to the standards that Bill had set for you, you kept your place.

At this moment, I accepted the Tottenham team were playing very well. The results were good and Bill did not need to change the side, but reserve-team football was no good to me. I decided that now was the time to have it out with Nicholson.

I knew when I sat down and faced Bill across the table, he would be totally honest with me. He wouldn't try to sweeten the pill. He would make no false promises in order to keep me happy. He would be straight and to the point. I would know exactly where I stood. It was decision time. Unfortunately for me, when it came to Spurs team affairs, only Bill's decision counted. Nicholson wasted no time spelling it out.

'The team's playing too well to make changes,' said Bill. 'You will have to play in the reserves and wait and see what happens. Maybe an injury could change things. You have to be patient.'

What Bill said came as no surprise. I could have written his script, but I saw it slightly differently to Bill, and now it was my turn to put my point across.

'I think, Bill, you could pick me as a sub for the next game,' I said. 'Bring me on for the last ten minutes of the game – a pair of fresh legs. Get me back playing at the top level.'

Nicholson jumped in and cut me short. He wasn't happy. 'I don't do that, Alan,' snapped Bill. 'I'm not sentimental. There's no room for sentiment in professional football.'

I didn't agree. I believed my request was both sensible and reasonable. I wasn't asking Nicholson for a favour; I was asking for a chance – the chance to prove myself. Football's all about confidence, and I was confident I could do a job for Spurs, but it was clear Nicholson didn't see it that way. He was being honest with me and I was being just as honest when I said, 'Reserve-team football is no good to me, Bill. I'm not playing there for the rest of the season.'

Bill didn't interrupt, he still listened, so I went on. 'I've heard Fulham have shown an interest in me.'

This time Bill did interrupt: 'I'm not selling you, Alan. You're not getting a transfer. You're not leaving Spurs. That's the end of it.'

But it wasn't the end. I carried on: 'What about a loan to Fulham?'

Bill got up. 'I'll have a word with the directors and come back to you.'

And that was the end of the meeting. When I left the office, I had mixed feelings. I was thankful Nicholson had been totally honest. There were no half-promises to raise hopes. I knew exactly where I stood: I did not figure in Bill's plans. But I believed eight years of doing the business in the first team and still being Alf Ramsey's first choice for England justified a subs role. My heart was still with Tottenham, but playing in the Spurs reserves to the end of the season wasn't for me. First-team football over at Craven Cottage with Fulham, however, was.

Nicholson wasted no time. He realised I was unhappy and he didn't like unhappy players around. It was all fixed – the next day I was off to Craven Cottage on a month's loan.

'You're still a Tottenham player,' said Bill, as I left for Fulham. 'And you're still the Spurs captain. Nothing's changed. It's a month's loan – let's see what happens.'

There was no 'good luck' from Nicholson, or even a 'keep in touch'. We had both been in the game long enough to know football's a funny game, full of the unexpected, and a month's loan in football is a very, very long time.

One week followed the next and I had heard nothing from Nicholson and my month's loan at Craven Cottage was coming to an end. The enforced rest because of my stomach strain, which was now completely healed and thankfully a thing of the past, and the games I'd played in the Spurs reserves, meant I was disgustingly fit and able to play for Fulham at the level I always demanded of myself. I was at home sitting in my favourite chair reading the paper when the phone rang. I decided to continue my read and let it ring. If it was important, they could call back. But it kept ringing, so I picked it up.

'Alan, it's Bill. How was the game?' came the voice on the other end of the line.

I smiled; nothing had changed. There was no small talk; Bill was straight to the point and it was good to hear his voice again.

'It went well, Bill,' I said.

Nicholson came back: 'Charlie Faulkner has seen you play your last two games. He reported to me, "It's the old Mullery." You're back playing at your best.'

All this was news to me. I never had an inkling that Charlie Faulkner (Tottenham's chief scout), had been watching me – but even if I had known, it would have made no difference to my performance. Once I pull a shirt over my head, no matter what the colour, I give everything. I want to win. It's my nature.

'That's right, Bill,' I said. 'I'm really enjoying my football. I'm playing well.'

'Good,' said Nicholson. 'Pick up your boots tomorrow and get over to Tottenham.'

That was it! I put the phone down. Bill, as always, had been brief and to the point. He had made a decision – I was to go back to Tottenham – and I acted on it. There was no welcoming committee on my return back to White Hart Lane and I did not expect to see one, and when I saw Nicholson I did not say, 'thanks for bringing me back'. Bill wouldn't have sought or expected a thank you. All Bill wanted to hear was that I was fully fit. I said I was.

'Good,' said Bill. He never once mentioned Fulham or the four weeks I had been away. He acted as if it had never happened. That's why there was no welcome back. In Bill's mind, I had never been away. He had simply carried on as normal. Tottenham had a UEFA Cup semi-final against AC Milan to play and nothing else was on Bill's mind.

I had hardly had time to draw my breath at Tottenham when Bill said, 'You're in the team against AC Milan and you're captain.'

Bill then gave me the long, unblinking Nicholson look which clearly spelt out: now it's all down to you, Mullery. Go out and show you deserve to be back.

I didn't need the Nicholson eyeball-to-eyeball challenge. I was up for it. Already, the adrenalin was pumping. I was busting to get out there.

I couldn't wait for the kick-off. I was back in the team and I was determined to prove to everyone I was back to stay.

Nicholson was as meticulous as ever: even more so as he covered the strengths and weaknesses of the AC Milan team. If he thought it was necessary, he would emphasise certain tactical points twice. Baily was even more passionate and animated than normal as he, in his own inimitable style, demanded a performance. Each and every one of us sitting in the dressing-room were left in no doubt as to what was expected of us out there during the game.

When I led the team out onto the pitch, the 42,000 crowd packed into the White Hart Lane ground let out an unbelievable roar and chanted 'RA-RA-RA-MUL-LER-Y' over and over again. I had no doubts I was now officially back.

'The Tottenham crowd,' said Nicholson later, 'were delighted that Mullery was back in the team. They loved skill but they also demanded hard work, and that's exactly what Mullery gave them.'

The last words Nicholson said to me as I left the dressing-room were, 'I want 90 minutes.' He kept repeating that I had to stay in control. There were to be no emotional outbursts, which, in the past, had got me my marching orders. Nicholson was only too aware that my opposite number in the Milan team, Sogliano, with his off-the-ball needling tactics, would test my temperament to the full.

The game got off to the worst possible start. Milan, thanks to a Benetti goal, went ahead, and with too many niggling fouls it quickly developed into a very physical and bad-tempered match. Sogliano was, as Nicholson predicted, doing his best to light the Mullery fuse, but I would have none of it. This was 1972; I had been through it all before, including playing in the 1970 World Cup in Mexico. Like the rest of the Tottenham lads, I was too busy giving everything and more as we battled to get level – and we did, when Steve Perryman, from just outside the box, fired in a cracker of a goal, and that's how it stayed until half-time.

The second half followed the same pattern. The repeated fouls continued to break up the rhythm of play. Then the red card, that Nicholson believed would end my encounter with Sogliano, was raised, and Nicholson was to get exactly what he wanted: his full 90 minutes from his captain. Sogliano was given his marching orders. Then Perryman scored Spurs' second goal – another tremendous long-range effort – and that goal was good enough for Tottenham to win the game 2–1.

Back in the dressing-room, we counted the bruises. It had been a hard match and we were glad we had won the battle, but we also accepted we had not won the war. Away goals counted as two in the event of a draw. It was going to be tough to win through in Milan.

'We'll see who the big men are out there,' I heard myself saying, speaking my thoughts aloud, and Nicholson, who said nothing at the time, admitted later that he agreed.

'Mullery was right,' said Nicholson. 'It was going to be a night for players with character, and Mullery was one I would need more than most.'

It's always great to read the papers after you win, and I enjoyed Jeff Powell's report in the *Daily Mail*. Jeff knows his football; he's one the players read because he always gives a balanced report of a game. I put this report aside and kept it. Jeff's words were praise indeed, and they went like this:

> The way Tottenham battled was also a tribute to the returning Alan Mullery, who gave Spurs renewed drive and direction.
>
> It was much to do with Mullery's urging that Spurs forced surprising cracks in one of the world's greatest defences.

Nice one, Jeff!

The return leg in Italy produced a very tense and very nervy dressing-room, but it was also a confident one. The lads were up for it. Nicholson made it very clear what he expected from each of us on the night, with a warning to keep our heads. We had to stay out of the referee's notebook, no matter what.

Back at White Hart Lane, after the first leg, I had opened my mouth in the dressing-room and said, 'We'll see who the big men are.' Now I had to go out and prove it.

The roar, followed by mile-high flares, exploding smoke bombs, whistling rockets and fire crackers set off by the 70,000 Italians in the San Siro stadium, was unbelievably loud – deafening – but it was in no way intimidating. The Tottenham lads had an unshakeable belief that it would be our night.

Nicholson knew, we all knew, that an early goal would silence the crowd and Milan would have to score three goals to win – a target that, we believed, would be beyond them. Usually, when you kick off in a game, the rush of adrenalin levels out after a few minutes, but this night was different. I was still well pumped up when, with the game seven minutes old, Steve Perryman laid off the perfect sideways pass. I didn't have to alter my running path or my stride, nor did I have to check my pace or steady myself. Thanks to Perryman, all I had to do was hit the ball, and I did just that. I've belted a few balls in my time, but I've never connected with the power I produced this night. The strike was perfect. Bang, in the sweet spot. I knew the moment the ball left my foot, Tottenham had got the all-important early goal. Later, the photograph in the Spurs programme of my goal showed the ball just as it left my foot and it was shaped more like a rugby ball. It was almost oblong, such was the power put into the shot. I had never hit a ball better or with more intent.

Although Rivera converted a dubious penalty – Phil Beal swore he won the ball fairly and Bignon dived over his legs – it didn't matter; I was never worried. We were always in control and Tottenham had little trouble winning 3–2 on aggregate. Back in the dressing-room, everyone, and that included Bill Nicholson, was delighted that we were in a European final.

Nicholson came over and I said, 'I've scored a few good goals in my time, Bill, but that one must rate as the most valuable ever.'

Bill agreed. He had a big smile on his face, but his eyes still gave a look that demanded even more. He realised I was on a roll and he wanted to keep the roll going, and I went along with that. I also wanted more.

Hunter Davies, in the now cult *The Glory Game* book, in which he never pulled his punches, wrote on that night in Milan:

'Mullery's goal was one of those which come at the perfect psychological moment. And with the scorer being Mullery, the prodigal returned, it was indeed like a story straight out of the *Wizard* or *Hotspur.*'

I agreed with Hunter: it was comic book stuff, but I didn't feel like a comic book hero. There were hard matches to be played, games to be won, and football doesn't always throw up a fairy-tale ending.

For once, Nicholson could not hide his delight. Now, after more years than he would like to remember, Tottenham were in another European final.

Sir Alf Ramsey then stepped into the picture. I was selected for the England squad. Nicholson was right; I was on a roll and I had to keep it going.

Wolves beat the Hungarian team Ferencvaros in the other semi-final, and, for the first time, two English teams were to meet over two legs in a European Cup final. It was a different atmosphere travelling up the M6 to Wolverhampton – instead of somewhere in Europe – to play the first leg of the UEFA Cup final. On paper, Tottenham and Wolves might have looked like a league game. We were playing against players we knew well, like the unpredictable and highly talented Derek Dougan and the equally dangerous Wagstaffe, Richards and Hegan: all goal-takers and goal-makers in a Wolves side which had scored 25 goals on their way to the final.

In the dressing-room, Nicholson and Baily were acutely aware of the dangers the Wolves players posed. They were not telling us to go out and play high-risk football – this was the away leg – but they both wanted a win on the night; none more so than Baily, who had the last word as we left the dressing-room: 'Win tonight and we've won the Cup.'

Both teams had chances in the first half – not good chances but they were chances, which, on another night, might well have gone in. It was a Mike England free-kick and the head of Chivers that put Spurs ahead, but Wolves hit back with a free-kick of their own. This time, Richards picked out McCalliog, who put Wolves level. With three minutes to go, a draw away in a two-legged tie was, for Tottenham, an acceptable result, but the words of Baily were still ringing in my head.

At this moment, I had the ball, and my first reaction was to go forward, get up to their box, have a crack, get the goal and win the match, but instinctively I found myself hitting the ball across field to Chivers, whom I had spotted standing on his own. I have never delivered a cross-field pass better. Chivers collected the ball, raced forward and, from fully 30 yards, let fly. The ball fairly whistled into the net. It was easily the best of the 40-odd goals big Chivers had scored that season.

Back in the dressing-room, Baily was ecstatic with the win. Nicholson, as always, was emotionally unmoved. He was, however, very pleased with the result, and every one of the Spurs lads was happy too. Before the game, I had written to Sir Alf Ramsey asking not to be considered for future international matches. I reckoned that, at 30, it was doubtful I would make the England World Cup team for 1974 so it was time to step down and spend more time with the family.

Sandwiched between our two-legged UEFA Cup final with Wolves was an away match with Arsenal. The games against Arsenal meant a lot to Bill. He would march into the first players' meeting at pre-season training and say, 'Right, this season I want to win this, this and this, AND beat Arsenal home and away.' That was how important it was to Bill. If we were only going to win two games in a season, they had to be the two against Arsenal. Possibly, this deep, all-consuming desire to beat Arsenal dated back to Bill's playing days in the '50s. In the last two games Bill played for Spurs against Arsenal, they were beaten 4–0 away and 4–1 at home. Players never forget big, embarrassing defeats – they stand alongside your memories of the glory nights.

As for me, I always considered the Spurs v. Arsenal derby game as one of the real high-points of the season. It was a different ball game to the West London derbies between Fulham and Chelsea. The North London derby was more intense, with a much sharper rivalry altogether.

Arsenal had just lost the FA Cup final – Leeds beat them 1–0 – so they were obviously determined to lift their fans with a win against Spurs. It would be another tough match. The players want to win these games just as much as the supporters, but even taking all that on board, I believed nobody wanted to win these matches more than Nicholson.

So it was a very happy Mullery who bounced into the dressing-room at full-time. Tottenham had beaten Arsenal 2–0 and I had scored one of the goals. Nicholson was delighted, it was a good team effort, but there was no pat on the back for the goal I had scored and I didn't expect one. But, as I caught Nicholson's eye, I said, 'Another goal, Bill.'

Nicholson looked at me. He didn't fall for the bait and say, 'Yes, well done, Alan.' Instead, he walked over and said, 'Save one for the final.'

I had to smile. I even had a little laugh. That was what made

Nicholson such a successful manager. He was always demanding more – not for himself, but for Tottenham.

It was just six weeks since my return to Tottenham from my loan period with Fulham. In that time, Spurs had not lost a match and we still had to keep the run going. Although it was widely accepted, following our 2–1 win in the first leg in Wolverhampton, that the UEFA Cup was already on the Tottenham sideboard, we knew only too well the way the Wolves side had played in the first game at Molineux. We still had plenty to do now in the return at White Hart Lane. As in the return-leg semi-final against AC Milan, we were all aware if we scored first, they would have to get three goals to beat us.

I looked across at Nicholson in the dressing-room on the night of the match. He nodded back; nothing was said. He recognised I was all pumped up ready to play the game of my life. No words were necessary.

Wolves began well and a couple of times they threatened the Tottenham goal. The early goal we were looking for hadn't come. Then, 15 minutes before half-time, Tottenham were awarded a free-kick and Martin Peters stepped up to take it. Peters was in a class of his own at knocking in a free-kick that would invite the goalkeeper to come, but then bend away out of his reach at the very last moment, and this proved to be one of those nights when the ball did exactly that.

I watched Peters closely as he took the kick. I judged the ball's flight. I thought 'right, it's mine', but as I raced in, I realised the Wolves goalkeeper had gone early. He was favourite: the ball was his. So I dug a little deeper, striving to lengthen each stride, and then, as I saw the goalkeeper go for the ball, I took off and threw myself through the air. My head met the ball and then I knew nothing else. I landed face down – my face buried in the ground. I scored, but had been knocked out by a big fist in the air, which I hadn't seen at all. I was brought round by the noise of the cheering crowd. We had scored first and we had the early goal. David Wagstaffe went on to get one back for Wolves, but one was not enough. Spurs had won the UEFA Cup.

After the match, it was party time in the Spurs dressing-room – one big celebration – but I missed out on the champagne. The Spurs players pushed me out of the dressing-room for a one-man parade round White Hart Lane holding the Cup! The Tottenham crowd that had invaded the pitch patted my head, slapped me on the back, lifted me up in the air and kept chanting 'MULLERY, MULLERY, MULLERY'. It was unbelievable madness, but I loved every minute of it and I never once let go of the Cup, even though it weighed a ton.

Nicholson did not come out to acknowledge the cheering Tottenham crowd. He stayed in the dressing-room. He had another European Cup to place on the Tottenham sideboard. This, for Nicholson, was classed as just 'satisfaction', because Tottenham had not won in style. It lacked 'enjoyment'.

During the welcomed summer break, I had time to sit back and reflect on the unbelievable and successful time I had enjoyed on my return to Tottenham following my month's loan at Fulham. After much thought, and even more soul-searching, I made a decision. I decided that now was the time to leave Tottenham. I had made the choice to leave the England team when Sir Alf Ramsey still believed I had a role to play. I left with nothing but good memories. The timing was right; I still have those good memories. I now felt the same way about Tottenham. I was happy with the European medal I had won and was filled with nothing but glorious, happy memories, thanks to Nicholson, Baily, the Spurs players, the supporters – everything about wonderful White Hart Lane. It was one long, happy memory. That was how I wanted it to remain. My mind was firmly made up; it was now time to leave Tottenham.

Funnily enough, when I told Nicholson of my decision and he agreed to let me go, I might, if he had tried to get me to stay, have changed my mind. It took a lot to turn your back and walk away from Bill Nicholson.

* * *

Prior to the second-leg of that final of the 1972 UEFA Cup, my co-author, Paul Trevillion, spoke to Bill Nicholson, Pat Jennings and Phil Beal while preparing his regular column in *The Sunday People*. Here, Paul remembers his conversations with Bill, Pat and Phil as he went about previewing the final, and Pat Jennings in 2005 talks about his memories of Nicholson during his days at Tottenham.

Pat Jennings on Bill Nicholson

'Tottenham's Pat Jennings offers forwards no encouragement,' said Gordon Banks. 'He doesn't give away silly goals. He's unflappable under pressure and keeps out shots he has no right to. I am the first to admit that this big Irish lad is the most consistent goalkeeper in the league.'

I thanked Banks for his very honest opinion of the Pat Jennings goalkeeping craft and I told him to get *The Sunday People*: it would all be in there and he would enjoy the read.

A couple or so weeks later, I was talking to Pat Jennings about Tottenham's chances in the return leg of the 1972 UEFA Cup final and Pat was modest enough to check if Gordon Banks had actually said those words to me.

'Every single word,' I told Pat, who then went on to praise the goalkeeping skills of Banks. I listened – I would use it another day – but now I wanted to know if Derek Dougan, who failed to score in the first leg at Molineux, could get the goals to win the UEFA Cup for Wolves.

'When I was a 17 year old playing for Watford in the Third Division,' said Jennings, 'Derek Dougan frightened the life out of me. He'd say, "I'm sticking four past you today, Jennings," but he never did. In fact, I've played against Dougan 20 times and his only goal was a deflection off a defender. But I still treat Doog with respect. He's tremendous in the air, crafty, with all the skills. If he could tank a ball like Chivers, he'd be the greatest centre-forward of all time.'

Jennings was confident about Spurs chances: 'Because away goals count double, our 2–1 win at Molineux means Wolves have got to knock two past me to stand any chance of lifting the UEFA Cup. It's just not on, if our defence plays as well as they did up there.'

I asked Pat what was the tactical defensive plan in the first leg that kept Dougan, Richards and Wagstaffe off the score-sheet.

'You'd better ask Phil Beal,' said Pat. 'He's the best one to talk to you about that. Let me give you his phone number.'

I phoned Phil Beal and he was very helpful with an expert tactical analysis on how the Tottenham defence did their job in the away game at Molineux.

'Up at their place,' said Beal, 'Mike England marked Dougan,

Knowles marked Richards and Kinnear marked Wagstaffe. My job was to sweep up at the back. It worked a treat. It'll be different at Tottenham. We'll be looking for another goal to settle it, so our defensive formation will probably mean me picking up Richards, with Knowles the spare man, free to attack down the wing. If Kinnear plays Wagstaffe as well as he did up there, we'll go a long way to eliminate Dougan. He relies a lot on Waggy's crosses. I'll have to watch Richards closely, because he is always liable to stick out a foot and plonk one in. It'll be danger when Hegan gets the ball; he's got a tremendous brain, always testing a defence with first-time balls into space and long, accurate upfield punts to the strikers. But next Wednesday night, the best forward on the park will be ours – Chivers. And I'm sure he'll add one to the couple he got at Molineux. That can only mean one thing: the UEFA Cup for Spurs.'

I thought Beal had possibly given away one or two trade secrets, and if he had, it was down to me to protect him, so I phoned Bill Nicholson to check if he was happy for this illustrated technical analysis on the Wolves game to go in the *Sunday People*. It was a short conversation. 'I didn't think Beal listened,' said Bill, when I read over the words. I could tell Nicholson was impressed to discover he had such an attentive, plus retentive, defender in the Spurs team.

'The lad's got it right,' went on Bill, 'but we could change it on the night.'

I quickly picked up the conversation: 'Perryman and Mullery – what part will they . . .'

Nicholson interrupted: 'You should have asked Beal when you were talking to him. You would have saved yourself a phone call. Enjoy the match.'

And with that, down went the phone.

I didn't expect to get any inside information from Bill on Tottenham's game plans for the Wolves match, but at least I tried. I did get what I was looking for, though: the go ahead. The Beal article would be published with Bill's consent and, thanks to Bill, it had, as always, turned out to be a very cheap call.

On the night of the match at White Hart Lane, Jennings was at his magnificent best, and he again stopped Dougan from adding to his one-deflected-goal tally. Beal was also a tower of strength in the Tottenham

THE CUP'S COMING TO SPURS

"When I was 17, playing for Watford in the Third Division, Derek Dougan frightened the life out of me. He'd say 'I'm sticking four past you today, Jennings'—but he never did. In fact, I've played against Dougan 20 times and his only goal was a deflection off a defender."
PAT JENNINGS, Spurs.

DOUGAN

"But I still treat Doog with respect. He's tremendous in the air, crafty, with all the skills. If he could tank a ball like Chivers he'd be the greatest centre-forward of all time."

"Because away goals count double, our 2—1 win at Molineux means Wolves have got to knock two past me to stand any chance of lifting the E.U.F.A. Cup. It's just not on if our defence play as well as they did up there."

Spurs sweeper Phil Beal agrees with Jennings: "Up at Wolves, England took Dougan, Knowles took Richards and Kinnear took Wagstaffe. My job was to sweep up at the back—it worked a treat."

RICHARDS   DOUGAN   WAGSTAFFE

KNOWLES   ENGLAND   KINNEAR
           BEAL

Sunday People, 1972

defence, which restricted the rampant Wolves attack to one goal. It was not enough for Wolves, thanks to a brave Mullery 'knock out' goal. The game ended in a 1–1 draw and Tottenham had won the UEFA Cup just as Jennings and Beal had predicted.

After the game, Nicholson praised Jennings, which came as no surprise to Mullery, who was the Spurs captain and goal-scorer that night.

'Bill rated Jennings very highly,' confirmed Mullery. 'Even so, like all of us he didn't get a lot of praise, but I believed he got more than most and it was deserved. He was easily the best goalkeeper around.'

It's generally accepted down at White Hart Lane that Jennings and Nicholson had a very good working relationship, one built on mutual respect, and Jennings in 2005 talked about it:

'Bill Nicholson's great strength was his coaching. When preparing me for a match, he would cover every aspect of the forthcoming game. He was meticulous. He would brief me on what to expect from the opposition's forwards: who was good in the air, what was their strong foot, who was fast around the pitch, what might happen at a free-kick, who would take the penalties and what side of the goal they usually went for. He would send me out into battle very well prepared.

'When I first joined Spurs from Watford as a teenager, Bill found it very hard-going with me, because he was not a goalkeeper, and in those days goalkeeping coaches were very thin on the ground. I didn't know what was required; it was a totally new world for me: a real baptism of fire. Now, keepers are surrounded by specialist coaches, but then it was just Bill Brown and myself and basically we were rivals for the first-team jersey. For me, it was all one big learning process, and under Bill's wing I had to learn fast.

'What was Bill's secret? Well, for me, I can sum it up in five words: he was down to earth. From day one, it was "call me Bill", and this put you at ease at once. You needed to feel at ease, because at that time Bill was a household name. He was a legend, up there with all the great managers. He should have been knighted. He should have been Sir Bill Nicholson: no doubt about it. But right from the start, it was "call me Bill".

'I had total respect for the man. Nobody at Tottenham took liberties with Bill Nicholson. Yes, it's true, Bill was a hard man to please, and quite often you didn't get given much credit. After the game, he always wanted to talk about the mistake I'd made and rarely the great save.

'One exception was in a UEFA Cup game in Zurich, Switzerland, against Grasshoppers. He walked into the dressing-room after the game, sat us all down and announced to the other players, "You can give your bonus to the goalkeeper tonight." Compliments like that were few and far between, but when they came they were probably much sweeter than if you were getting them every match.

'I was with Bill for ten years of my career, and he was like a father-figure to me. I found him to be the perfect boss. I have to give him ten out of ten. I have nothing but good to say about the man. He ran the club from top to bottom. He was Mr Tottenham. What Bill always preached was loyalty. Over the years, he gave just that to Tottenham, both as a player and a manager. After the slight blip when Bill and Spurs parted company in 1974, I have to say the club were very good to him and treated him very well in the years following. To sum up, I have just one thing to say: I was lucky indeed to have worked for such an honest and good man.'

CHAPTER TWELVE

Sir Bill Nicholson Campaign

One of the biggest injustices in football over the last 100 years was the fact that Bill Nicholson was never knighted for his services to the game. He is up there with the likes of Alex Ferguson, Bobby Robson and Alf Ramsey. They all received a knighthood, yet Nicholson didn't. He was a decent, honest man and it wouldn't have unduly bothered him; but it does bother us.

Yes, it's true, Bill was awarded an OBE, but, welcome as it was, it was not enough recognition. We aim to put this injustice right. Right here in the pages of this book we are starting the Mullery–Trevillion campaign to win Bill a posthumous award. We are seeking what is his ultimate right – a knighthood, no less – and it is not too late. We are saying let's campaign long and hard to be able to say Sir Bill Nicholson of Tottenham Hotspur Football Club.

It is hard to find one single reason why this honour should not sit on Bill's shoulders, even though he is no longer alive to enjoy all it means. The evidence in favour is overwhelming and we urge all Spurs fans and football fans in general to contact the ceremonial secretariat, Cabinet Office – the address is to be found at the end of this section – and to push for this honour for Bill. The Mullery–Trevillion push for justice for Bill begins here. We urge readers to act now.

Ten Good Reasons Why it Must be Sir Bill

1 **Loyalty to Tottenham**: Bill Nicholson joined as an apprentice in 1936, when his duties included just about any odd job around White Hart Lane. Between 1938 and 1955, he played as a wing-half for Spurs and, in 1958, went on to manage the club until 1974. He was club president from 1991 to 2004.

2 **His management record**: That has been well documented in these pages, but two achievements surely underline his qualification for a knighthood. In 1961, he became the first manager to lead his club to the FA Cup and league Double since Aston Villa in 1897. In 1963, he became the first manager to lead a British team to a European trophy when Spurs won the European Cup-Winners' Cup in Rotterdam.

3 **He stood for fair play and sportsmanship**: Bill played his football in a sporting manner and managed Spurs in the same way. He advocated Tottenham playing the game in a foul-free and fair way and detested any form of dirty tactics. If a Spurs player was sent off, he would receive little sympathy from Bill.

4 **He loved the fans**: Bill's overriding passion was to entertain the paying public. He would even take the side of the fans if he thought they were right in booing one of his Spurs players.

5 **He respected the referee**: 'Don't argue with the ref; he's never going to change his mind,' he told his Spurs players. That was hard advice to follow, but Bill was right.

6 **He was appalled by hooliganism**: So angry and upset was Bill by the growing threat of serious hooliganism in English football that it even contributed to his shock decision to quit the Spurs job in 1974. He didn't want any part of that – especially when it was Spurs fans misbehaving in Rotterdam in the 1974 UEFA Cup final.

7 **He served his country in the Second World War**: In the War, Bill served in the Durham Light Infantry as an infantry instructor and also as a physical training instructor.

8 **He played football for his country in peacetime**: Bill, when 32, won his only full England cap in 1951. He scored with his first kick against Portugal.

9 **He coached his country in a World Cup**: In 1958, Bill was part of Walter Winterbottom's England coaching team prior to the World Cup in Sweden.

10 **He put country before club**: Bill was always delighted when a Spurs player got an international call-up and would make sure that that player would be available to meet up with the squad. How different from today, where pressures on managers have made many think that international duty is a menace to the club's fortunes.

Where do you end? We are sure readers can find another 50 good reasons for Bill to get that posthumous knighthood.

On his death in 2004, many tributes were paid, but let us just remind readers of one from a football legend: Sir Bobby Robson. Sir Bobby said this in the *News of the World*: 'He was not only one of our great football managers, but also one of our great coaches: solid, honest and totally reliable.' How wonderful it would be if Sir Bobby can be joined by Sir Bill.

His legendary winger from the 1961 Double team, Cliff Jones, pointed the way when, again at the time of Bill's death, he said, 'I am amazed he wasn't given a knighthood. He did so much for the game and the community.' Cliff, you are not the only one who is amazed. Many feel the same way. It's time this changed and the road at White Hart Lane became Sir Bill Nicholson Way.

How You Can Nominate Bill

To nominate Bill for a posthumous knighthood, please write a letter of support expressing why you feel Bill deserves the honour and send it to:

Ceremonial Secretariat
Cabinet Office
35 Great Smith Street
London SW1P 3BQ
Tel: 020 7276 2777
E-mail: ceremonial@cabinet-office.x.gsi.gov.uk

Act now – remember that, in life, every 'no' takes you one step nearer a 'yes' – and the letter you send could be the one that gets Bill the posthumous knighthood he deserves.

* * *

Alan Mullery writes:

My record as a player was in no way exemplary. I was sent off on many occasions, including being the first England player to receive his marching orders. Yet I received the MBE for my services to football. Now, I am not saying it wasn't appreciated – it was – but when you consider what Bill Nicholson achieved in the game and the manner in which he did it, both as a player and a manager, he surely deserves much more than an OBE. Honesty, modesty and fair play were his trademark.

Let's look at some of the other managers who have been knighted. They all deserved the honour, but my firm belief is that Bill's long career in football surpassed Sir Bobby Robson and even surpassed Sir Alf Ramsey, and yet they were both knighted. Today, the likes of Matthew Pinsent and Steve Redgrave become Sirs for rowing success over 20-odd years. These honours were well deserved, I agree, but Bill was involved in football for over 50 years. He surely passes the test of time.

Bill Nicholson also passed the test of greatness at Tottenham, with flying colours. If you achieve greatness, and if awards are given for greatness in sport, then Bill should have got the greatest award: a knighthood.

I was in no way a saint when I played for Bill. When I stepped out of line, he would give me a massive dressing down. He knew I was not only hurting myself, but I was hurting the game of football and the name of Tottenham Hotspur Football Club, and Bill did not like that one little bit. He loved the game of football; he loved Tottenham Hotspur; he didn't want to see it hurt and he was prepared to stand up for it even if it meant reprimanding his own players. Bill did not want the name of Tottenham hurt in any way, both on and off the field. His attitude was that if you hurt the club, you hurt him personally. Tottenham Hotspur was his life.

I never actually heard Bill tell us, if we were deliberately and repeatedly kicked, not to retaliate. He didn't have to. We all knew, in Bill's book this was not the done thing. It was hard not to retaliate, but we accepted if we did, we would have Bill to answer to.

Bill's dedication to the game and Spurs is legendary. He had no hobbies, no small talk. He worked for the club every hour that God sent. His total dedication to the game and Spurs was frightening. It was so frightening – and I don't use that word lightly – that I decided when I was at Tottenham that I did not and would not become a manager. As a player, I rarely saw my family, and I reasoned that if Bill was the yardstick to go by, I was going to see even less of them if I went into management. I was there; I saw what Bill Nicholson did to make Spurs successful and I wasn't prepared to devote my whole life to that. Bill did, and it's another reason why he should be Sir Bill Nicholson.

How his wife, Darkie, lived with that all those years is quite remarkable. She was an absolute diamond. I asked her once how she coped and she said, 'Alan, football was Bill's life. Tottenham was his life. He asked for no more.'

Darkie accepted the situation and was happy to go along with it, and full marks to her. She was a very rare breed. Most wives would find Bill's sort of single-mindedness in his career impossible to live with.

To sum up, it was Bill's dedication to football that made the biggest overall impression on me during my Tottenham days. It is surely this dedication which makes him worthy of a posthumous knighthood.

* * *

Paul Trevillion writes:

Bill Nicholson achieved his success as a manager with a Tottenham team that played skilfully, fairly and in an entertaining fashion. Through all the glory years, Nicholson never changed. As a man, he was exactly the same young lad that started out at Tottenham: modest, decent, respectful and full of enthusiasm for the game of football. Few other men in football, living or dead, have portrayed such fine qualities as Nicholson did.

All in all, Nicholson was not a man of many words. He did not say a lot, but what he did say was always worth hearing. I believe it was Nicholson's integrity that spoke most for him. His principles never varied, and nor did his ideals, nor his faith in football and Tottenham Hotspur. He was a knight in shining armour. I believe, like every Tottenham fan, he deserves a posthumous knighthood.

Appendices

Nicholson Never Dropped his Guard: Don Revie in Conversation with Paul Trevillion

The Leeds United manager Don Revie had a tremendous respect for Bill Nicholson, but then Revie was a very respectful man. In all the years I knew him, he never once had a bad word to say about another manager or another team's player.

'There is no better judge of a player than Bill Nicholson,' Revie told me in 1972. 'He does his homework. He digs deep into the player's character and ability. He leaves no room for guesswork. Nicholson knows exactly what he wants in a player and he is never afraid to back his own judgement. His very few bad buys are well outweighed by the unbelievable number of great players he got to sign for him and then do the business at Tottenham.'

Revie smiled and went on: 'Nicholson fancies quite a few of my Leeds players. Johnny Giles is always top of his list. He's a great admirer of Giles, but he knows I would never sell him. Paul Madeley is another high on his list. Madeley is an unbelievable athlete. He has exceptional balance, a fine turn of speed and is an excellent short and long passer of a ball. In the air, Madeley not only wins the ball, he directs it to a teammate. Make no mistake about it, Madeley has all the tools. You can't play Madeley out of position, because he can play equally well in every position on the field, and he's done it for Leeds. To call Madeley a 'utility player' does an injustice to the man. He's the most versatile footballer I have seen in all my years in the game. But what is Madeley's best position? It's a question I still ask myself.' Revie laughed. 'When Nicholson phoned up about Madeley, I thought now is my chance to get the best judge of a player in the game to give me his opinion. Maybe Nicholson had the answer. Maybe he had spotted something in Madeley's game that we had missed at Leeds.

'"Where are you going to play him, Bill?" I asked.

'Nicholson came straight back: "In the first team."

'That was it. Nicholson never dropped his guard. I would have liked to have known the position Nicholson would have played Madeley, but he was keeping that to himself.

'There are lots of managers in the game who I regard as my friends, who I can talk things over with, but Nicholson is not one of them. In general, he keeps his opinions to himself. Like I say, Nicholson never drops his guard, but I respect him for that.'

I well remember my very first meeting with Don Revie back in 1965, which, as it proved, was the first of many. He was a tall man, so, although he was standing talking to three other gentlemen, it was easy for me to recognise the Leeds United manager. I was in the Europa Hotel, London, at the Sports Writers' Association's 17th Annual Dinner. The guest of honour was the prime minister Harold Wilson. The Sportsman of the Year was Tommy Simpson, the world professional road-race champion (cycling), and the Sportswoman of the Year was Marion Coakes, world show-jumping champion (equestrianism).

I waited until Revie was on his own, and then hurried over to collect his autograph and to congratulate him on the very successful season Leeds had enjoyed.

'Have you still got the two wooden elephants that Peter Lorimer gave you when he signed on for Leeds as a full-time professional?' I asked.

Revie laughed and answered the question with another question: 'How did you know about the two wooden elephants?'

It was time to introduce myself. 'My name is Paul Trevillion and I was the artist who did the drawings to illustrate your life story which appeared in strip form in the *Daily Express*. It was all in there about Lorimer.'

Revie sat down. I joined him and I continued the conversation. 'I did those drawings just two years ago, Don, and Leeds were in the Second Division. You did what you said you would do in the strip. You took Leeds up and, with a bit of luck, you could have done the Double last season.'

Revie jumped in. 'We lost the championship on goal difference and the Cup in extra-time. That's about as close as you can get without winning them. We deserved at least one.'

I nodded in agreement. 'Leeds proved the Double can be done again,' I said, and went on. 'I thought when my team, Tottenham, pulled off the Double, it would be years before it happened again.'

I was about to get up when I fired another question at Revie: 'You played against the Tottenham push-and-run team in the '50s that won the Second and First Division championships in consecutive seasons and you saw the Nicholson Double winners. Which did you rate the best?'

Revie didn't hesitate in answering: 'The best team was the '50s and the best players were in the Nicholson Double side.'

Before I could challenge Revie on that verdict, he went on: 'The '50s team did the simple things easily, quickly and accurately. The short-passing game is usually a slow build-up, but that Tottenham side moved the ball so quickly they cut through teams like a knife through butter.'

Revie was in full flow and I sat back, enjoying every minute.

'Their right-back, Ramsey, was an excellent player. What stopped him being one of the all-time greats was his lack of pace, but when it was called for he was the one who could hit a 40-yard pass and split a defence wide open. That Tottenham side was some team.'

I now wanted to tell Revie how good the rest of that team was – players like Ditchburn, Willis, Nicholson, Clarke, Burgess, Walters, Bennett, Duquemin, Baily and Medley – but Revie didn't pause for breath!

'Football's a simple game,' said Revie. 'You can write a book on how to be a footballer – kicking, heading, passing and all that – and you can write two books on systems and tactics, but if you are talking about how to play the *game* of football, it's one page and four sentences.'

Revie stopped talking, picked up my pen, which was on my folder ready for him to sign his autograph, and said, handing me the pen, 'Write this down. It's what was hammered into me day and night by Sep Smith when I joined Leicester. It's the way Nicholson likes to play and we do at Leeds.'

I started to write as Revie spelt it out:

> When not in possession, get into position.
> Never beat a man by dribbling if you can beat him with a pass.
> It's not the man on the ball, but the man running into position
> to collect the pass who is the danger.
> The aim is to have a spare man in the passing movement.

'That's all it is,' laughed Revie. 'Play your football this way and it's easy.'

I still wanted Revie's views on my Tottenham heroes of the '50s. 'How good was Ditchburn?' I butted in.

Revie laughed again. He had an infectious laugh. 'I would not have swapped him for our goalkeeper at Manchester City, Bert Trautmann. In my opinion, Trautmann has never had an equal, but Ditchburn played his part in the push-and-run side. Ditchburn was great at coming off his line and catching balls in the penalty area. He had great hands and was very agile, but surprisingly enough Ditchburn, who was a big man, couldn't kick a ball. Even when the ball was in his hands, he had trouble reaching the halfway line. So, when he had possession, he would roll the ball out to Ramsey or throw a short one to Nicholson or Burgess, or even a long one to someone like Baily. This meant he didn't give the ball away with an aimless kick down field. Thanks to Ditchburn's accurate throws, Tottenham kept possession and built up from the back.'

I was amazed how well Revie remembered the names of the push-and-run side, although I was to find out later he had a mental dossier on just about every player in the game. My next question was, 'How good were Nicholson and Burgess?'

Revie shook his head. 'Let's take Burgess first. When I was 19 playing for Leicester against Spurs, Burgess almost ended my career.

We both went for the ball and I finished up with my right ankle broken in three places. It was a complete accident. No blame on Burgess. As I lay there on the pitch waiting for the stretcher, Burgess, who was very upset, kept saying, "Take it easy, Don." He stood over me and kept repeating those words until I was carried off.

'As a player, Burgess had the lot. He could tackle, head the ball, pass it, score goals and he could move a bit. At his peak, he was head and shoulders above the rest of the Tottenham team. Before Ramsey arrived, Burgess was Tottenham and he was an automatic choice for Wales. He finished up with a pile of caps. Nicholson was capped once. He was unlucky. Billy Wright of Wolves, who was the England captain and the man in possession, never played a bad game for England. So Nicholson missed out, but only as a player. Looking back, I believe Nicholson was picked a record number of times as an England reserve, which meant he was able to spend time with Walter Winterbottom [who was the England manager and director of coaching]. Even in those days, Nicholson was heavily into coaching. He already had his full FA coaching badge.'

I wanted Revie to continue talking, but once or twice he had nodded to people who had passed our table and it was that unmistakable nod that indicates 'I will join you in a few minutes'. I knew at best I had one last question. 'Is Nicholson a better manager than he ever was a player?' I asked.

Revie, as I got to know him better, was an extremely polite man. He didn't have to continue the conversation. After all, we were not talking about his club, Leeds. 'I will just say this,' answered Don, as he picked up some paper from the table, his body language making it clear he was getting ready to leave. 'Nicholson, like Ramsey, was a little short of pace, but he could have given Ramsey a yard start in a hundred and beaten him, so he was no slow coach. At right-half, Nicholson was the player in front of Ramsey. Both of them had quick football brains, which meant a great understanding. During a game, they kept in close contact, and between them they would cut off any pass intended for the wing-forwards. Nicholson was a good ball-winner and he never 'sold' himself in a tackle. Unless it was a 50–50 ball, he would hold off and try to force the forward to part with it. When Nicholson did tackle, he went in very hard, but fairly. Ramsey, on the other hand, would stick a foot out and try to 'nick' the ball away. He never went into a tackle, so to speak. There was nothing physical about Ramsey – but you knew it when you were on the other end of a Nicholson tackle.'

Revie was now standing up, so I got up and made my way round to stand next to him as he continued talking. 'Because that Tottenham team were so good at running off the ball, when Nicholson or Ramsey had possession, they had plenty of options, but it was no good calling for the ball. You would never get the words out of your mouth. The pass would already be on its way and if your name was on the ball, you got it. In defence, Nicholson was very reliable. He never neglected his defensive duties. You rarely caught him out of position and he wasn't one to give the ball away. If you wanted to get the ball off Nicholson, you had to win it, but Ramsey was the one who could cut a defence to ribbons with a 40-yard pass.'

Revie gave me a big smile, and as he turned to leave, I said, 'Baily was also a good passer of the ball.'

Revie gave me the same look Pat Jennings had once given me when I sat in his car down at Tottenham. I had come to see him about a goalkeeping article for the *Sunday Times* and we had been talking for over two hours.

'I thought we were doing an article,' said Jennings. 'We've done enough talking to fill a book.'

I put my pencil down. 'You're right, Pat,' I said, 'but I finished the article an hour and a half ago. I just like talking about Tottenham!'

Jennings laughed and started up the car. I got out, but we had struck up a great friendship.

Revie made his escape on foot, but not before saying, 'Baily was one of the best first-time passers of a ball in the game. That's why he was capped so many times. But like the rest of those Tottenham players, he was essentially a team man. They were 11 players who played football the way it was meant to be played: simple and quick. Call them the Arthur Rowe push-and-run side or the give-and-go team, but for me those Tottenham lads played it the Sep Smith way.'

As Revie walked off, I handed him the menu and asked him to sign. 'There you go,' he said. 'That's two signatures you've got,' and Revie was gone.

Revie was right, for when I put the menu into my folder, I saw there was one in there already signed. He must have done that when I first sat down to talk to him.

Seven years later, I showed those two signed menus to Revie when I was sitting in his manager's office at Leeds United Football Club. It was 1972, the FA Cup centenary year.

'How's the ankle, Don?' As I sat facing him, Don just continued looking at me, so I carried on. 'The ankle Burgess broke, how is it?'

Revie was highly skilled at answering a question with a question.

'Have you been talking to Burgess?'

'Not recently,' I replied and carried on. 'It's some years since I last spoke to Burgess and he was still talking about Nicholson and the one-penny typewriter.'

Revie looked puzzled. 'What's that all about?' he asked.

This was my chance to tell a story about Tottenham, and the words poured out. 'It was when the Tottenham team was playing away and Burgess was called to the phone to talk to a local press man,' I explained. 'Burgess was the Tottenham captain and the reporter wanted his views on the team, adding there would be a nice cheque waiting for him when he went to the ground.'

Revie obviously liked football stories. He was smiling, keen to hear more, so I carried on. 'Burgess gave the interview and all the time he was talking on the phone he could hear the typewriter pounding away above the usual office noises. The next day, Burgess arrived at the ground and was handed an envelope with his name on. When he opened it, he found a postal order for just six pence. Burgess was furious and he started sounding off in the dressing-room, but before it got completely out of hand, Nicholson, Ernie Jones and Freddie Cox, who, by then, were laughing their heads off, told Burgess they had gone into a call box and one of them did the interview acting as the reporter. Another tapped on the glass with a coin to make it sound like a typewriter and the office noises were created by moving and opening and shutting the telephone book. Burgess fell about. He enjoyed the joke.'

Revie's laugh was suddenly cut short. He was deadly serious. 'I would never have believed Nicholson would have been involved in a stunt like that. He must have a sense of humour,' said Don. 'In all the years I've known him, though, he's never shown it. Nobody really knows the man. He never drops his guard. We all know Nicholson the manager, but not the man. When you meet Nicholson, he talks football: only football. It's his only interest.' Revie shifted position in his chair as he prepared to make a point. 'Don't be fooled. Although Nicholson talks and talks football, his ears are never closed. He is listening to your every word. Now, think back to the great managers in the game Nicholson has been lucky to listen to. When he was a player: Arthur Rowe and Walter Winterbottom, the England manager. When he took over as Tottenham's manager, he had Danny Blanchflower, who had a very original and inventive football brain. As the Northern Ireland captain, Blanchflower played the major role with his revolutionary thinking and tactical innovations in taking the Irish side to the quarter-finals of the 1958 World Cup. With true Irish wit, Blanchflower would sum up his tactical leadership: "Our aim is to equalise before the other team scores."'

Revie laughed and went on: 'Blanchflower believed, and still does, in flexibility in team tactics. He argues that a change in team strategy could win a game as effectively as a brilliant piece of individual play. Nicholson was very brave and also very wise to have Blanchflower as the Tottenham captain. He accepted Blanchflower would also assume the role of manager if the game demanded. Blanchflower would listen and act on Nicholson's instructions from the bench, but if he felt the need and he had the courage of his beliefs, he would go with some of his own ideas and make tactical changes during a game. I'm not saying that Nicholson was happy with every decision that Blanchflower put upon himself to make during critical stages of a game, but I'm sure to a degree he never discouraged this adventuresome streak in Blanchflower's nature. There were times when it won games for Tottenham.'

Revie continued, 'Blanchflower and Nicholson were an unlikely team, as different as chalk and cheese in personalities, but when it came to talking football, they spoke the same language. They both wanted to win, but they also wanted to win in style.'

Revie then made his point: 'Nicholson has talked to just about every top manager in the game, and he always goes to school. He listens; he wants to learn. He's done the Double, won in Europe and has the Cups, and still he is the first one to tell you he doesn't know it all. That's the secret of Nicholson's success: he is football's best listener. You don't have to agree with everything that Nicholson has to say about football, but you are forced to admire his total dedication to the game.'

Revie sat back in his chair and quickly changed the subject. 'Terry Cooper. You've been talking to Terry Cooper. What's it all about?'

Terry Cooper was the England and Leeds left-back and he was the one who had asked me to travel up to Leeds and meet Revie. 'Have a look at this, Don,' I said. I handed him a piece of paper of a drawing I had done of a football-stocking tab – a small piece of leather with a player's number on it and a small piece of tape attached to it, for the player to tie up his sock.

'Before the game, they sign the backs of these stocking tabs,' I explained. 'Then, when the final whistle blows, they give them out to the crowd.'

Revie handed me back the piece of paper with my drawing on. 'I don't understand,' said Revie. 'What's the purpose?'

It was a long story, so I started at the beginning. This was my second sell-in of the pre-match football promotion I had dreamt up in America when I was introduced to baseball watching the Cleveland Indians in action. I enjoyed the game, but it was the unbelievable family atmosphere in the stadium that made the biggest impression. I remember thinking that Nicholson, who insisted it was the fans, not the players, who were the most important people at a club would, if he had been sitting next to me, have been just as impressed. I went to most sporting events in America: baseball, basketball, grid-iron football and even soccer, and always I was impressed by the family atmosphere and the fun promotions which, at times, included the star players. On my return to England, I started to work on ideas for a family-fun promotion, with Tottenham and Nicholson in mind.

The day I went down to Tottenham with my American-inspired pre-match ideas – stocking tabs, target balls and names on the players' shirts and tracksuits – doubts began to form in my mind. I became worried that Nicholson might not go along with it. The opinion of Danny Blanchflower that 'Nicholson is blinkered to everything outside of football' kept running and running around in my head. I had worked with Blanchflower on the same newspaper, the *Sunday Express*. One of my proudest possessions is a page dated 31 July 1966 that appeared in the paper which showed all the goals when England won the World Cup. On the same page is an accompanying article with Danny Blanchflower's views, and my name is printed alongside Blanchflower's. I had illustrated the Gary Player golf strip. That page, with all the signatures of the 1966 winning team, I keep in a very safe place.

'When Ramsey said Martin Peters was ten years ahead of his time,' I reminded Blanchflower when we met in the *Express* offices, 'he made Peters a star overnight. Nicholson needs to sell the present Tottenham side. Like Bill Shankly at Liverpool and Malcolm Allison at Manchester City, he has to tell the press how good the players are and make stars of them.'

Blanchflower spoke up for Nicholson: 'You will never get Nicholson to stand on a soapbox and sell the Tottenham players. He will tell you it's not his job. All the talking must be done by the players on the pitch. It's up to them to go out on a Saturday with their skills, demand the fans' applause and earn their star billing by showing just how good they are.'

Blanchflower continued, 'Nicholson encourages his players to express themselves and play open, attacking football which entertains the fans. It's the perfect platform for a player to make a name for himself. Nicholson will never be one of those managers who sells newspapers. He's never going to tell the press how good his players are. He doesn't even tell the players. It's the game on a Saturday with the players putting in a performance for the full 90 minutes and entertaining the fans that counts with Nicholson. He's blinkered to everything outside of football.'

I didn't argue with Blanchflower, but the baseball fan I sat next to when I watched the Cleveland Indians play would have put up a fight. 'I love all the entertainment,' I said to him as the baseball sailed into the crowd and the fireworks were let off and the fanfare of music blared out. 'We don't get this at our soccer grounds back in England.'

Most Americans need little encouragement to talk, and the baseball fan next to me proved no exception. 'When we come to a game, we want a fun day out. We want to be entertained, but you can't always guarantee that with sport. Go to the movies, the theatre or watch Elvis in concert and your entertainment is guaranteed. They're up there on

202

their own – no opposition; nothing to stop them performing – but it isn't like that in sport. There's another team or an opponent involved. Anything can happen.'

Having started the conversation, I felt obliged to listen, as between bites of his hotdog he powered on. 'All the fun and entertainment we have at our games ensures you have a great day out. Teams and even star players don't always do it on the day. Tell me how many zero–zero games . . .'

I interrupted: 'You mean goal-less games?'

He agreed, 'That's right. How many goal-less games are classics? Matches which are shown over and over again on TV?'

I sat there in silence. I couldn't remember one goal-less draw that had gone down in football history.

The baseball fan laughed, 'I proved my point. You can't tell me one goal-less game that was a classic. Dull, boring games where nothing happens we can accept, because we've not been cheated out of our entertainment and fun. The entertainment is a bonus when we win and a sweetener when we lose.'

How would Nicholson have reacted to all that? Very shortly, I was about to find out.

As always, Nicholson listened. He was politely quiet as I repeated over and over again how the Tottenham fans would love to be entertained with pre-match promotions, especially the autographed stocking tabs. 'The players will have worn those tabs for the entire game,' I said as I continued to paint the picture. 'Imagine it. Those tabs will be autographed and covered with the Tottenham grass and mud collected during the game. What a memory to take home.'

Nicholson had heard enough. 'It's not for me,' he said.

'But what . . .' I wasn't allowed to finish the sentence.

'It's not for me,' repeated Nicholson, more firmly. 'No – it's not for me.'

That was it. When Nicholson says no, he's not one to change his mind.

'Why don't you go and see Revie at Leeds?' came back Nicholson. 'They could do with it.'

I nodded, said thanks and started to walk away.

'I mean it,' went on Nicholson. 'Go and see Revie at Leeds. They're the team that need it.'

It was well documented that Nicholson was not an admirer of the way that Leeds played. He believed they were too physical, indulged in too much gamesmanship and were not an entertaining side to watch.

'They've got a good manager in Revie,' went on Nicholson. 'Cooper, Clarke, Madeley, Giles, Bremner . . . go through the side. They can all play a bit.'

I listened as Nicholson went on praising Revie and the Leeds team. I couldn't believe what I was hearing. Then, the sting in the tail. Nicholson hammered home his point. 'Leeds need to entertain more. They don't need all the physical stuff and the gamesmanship. They're too good a side.'

I kept running Nicholson's words over and over again in my head as I travelled home, and every time I came back to the Burgess 'penny typewriter' episode. Was Nicholson having a joke on me?

I had devised and drawn a couple of football articles with the Leeds defender Terry Cooper that had appeared in the *Sunday Times* and *Sunday People*. They were both very highly praised, thanks to Terry Cooper, who had an excellent football brain and the vocabulary to put his views together. Maybe, I reasoned, it would be a bit too ambitious trying to get Don Revie, the Leeds manager, to go along with my ideas, but a Leeds player who was an England international like Terry Cooper, who Revie had described as 'the best attacking defender or defensive attacker in the game', could do it on his own, become a superstar, a role model, and then other players would follow.

I phoned Terry Cooper and arranged to meet him the next time Leeds played a London club.

'Don likes us in bed by ten o'clock the night before a match,' said Cooper. 'So make it around eight o'clock.'

I agreed.

Adam Faith, actor and pop star, came along. I had been working with Leo Sayer at the time and Adam was to help with the Terry Cooper star image.

'I really want to do it all,' said Cooper when we did meet up. 'But Leeds are a family team. It's one for all and all for one. I'm not going to do it without the rest of the boys.'

Adam Faith decided to pass.

Terry Cooper was a very likeable lad and a tremendous football talker and he could see that pre-match entertainment could work at Leeds. I thought if the rest of the team were anything like him, I had a chance.

Revie had listened, never once saying a word except for 'carry on', when he went to break in at the mention of Nicholson's name.

'What about it then, Don?' I was eager for an answer.

'You don't need a yes from me,' responded Revie. 'You must see the boys. If they say yes, I'm on for it.'

I was happy and I added, 'What about them coming out a quarter of an hour before kick-off and doing the exercise routine?'

Revie laughed: 'Yes, I love that. Why should they warm up in the dressing-room?'

I had come up with the Leeds exercise routine only that morning. I had to wait to see Revie, so I had watched the Leeds United team training. They were the fittest players I had ever seen. It was all explosive running, jumping and bending, with high kicks that touched the sky. I thought if the Leeds trainer, Les Cocker, could choreograph the exercises Busby-Berkeley-style and get the Leeds team to run out, split into four and perform in the four corners, it would send the Leeds crowd wild and create a roar as if a goal had been scored before the kick-off.

'Tell me,' challenged Revie, 'did Nicholson say all those things about Leeds, or did you add some of your own to help sell your ideas to me?'

'Every word was true, Don,' I repeated. 'Nicholson said you were a great manager. You had great players and a great team. Ask Nicholson yourself when you next see him.'

'I don't talk to Nicholson much,' said Revie. 'It's not Nicholson's fault. He often asks after me when he comes up with his Tottenham team, but I'm never around. I'm nearly always too busy. Maybe next time he comes up I'll talk to him,' said Revie, not too convincingly. 'Maybe.'

Revie looked at his watch: a sign that it was almost time to go. 'Football's changed a lot since Nicholson did the Double,' said a thoughtful Revie. 'And Nicholson agrees. Only the other day in the papers, he was saying there was nothing he would like better than a return to entertaining, attacking football. He believes the game is ruled by the fear of losing. Teams set out not to lose, instead of going out to win.'

I had read the same article, so I knew what was coming next.

'Nicholson would like somebody to brainwash everyone in football, including the supporters, and get them to accept that winning is not the be all and end all of the game. Well, that's never going to happen,' said Revie. 'Nicholson is on his own if he believes that entertaining, attacking football, win or lose, is what the fans want.' Revie looked at me. 'Come on, you're a lifelong Tottenham fan. Would you rather Tottenham play badly and won or entertained and lost?'

'Don,' I replied, 'I always want to watch Tottenham win in style. So I would rather "hear" that Tottenham had played badly and won – but not watch it.'

Revie laughed out loud.

'You would like to hear it, but not watch Tottenham play badly and win?'

I said, 'That's right, Don. I've been brought up on the push-and-run and the Double team: fast-flowing, ball on the ground, attacking, winning football. The fans demand that at Tottenham.'

Revie shook his head. 'Nicholson helps set those high standards, but now, even if he wanted to compromise, the fans won't let him and that, I'm afraid, is the cross he has to bear.'

'Nicholson's got broad shoulders,' I came back. 'He's been involved in two record-breaking teams that played entertaining, attacking football. Why not a third? If anyone can do it, Nicholson can.'

Revie smiled. 'Dream on, dream on,' was all he said.

When I met the Leeds lads, I was impressed by their very friendly and highly professional attitude when, as a team, they sat and listened. They liked the stocking tabs and were willing to give the pre-match exercise routine a go. Big Jack Charlton – who I got to like a lot: the man was solid gold – was the key to the exercise routine. Revie warned me that the whole promotion would hang on Jack. He doubted he would go for it, especially the high kicks, but Charlton saw the rest of the lads were keen so he gave it the thumbs up. The pre-match promotion was on.

Nicholson was right to point me in the direction of Leeds, but when he gave me that advice he did not know that fate would intervene and his Tottenham team would be drawn to play Leeds at home in the FA Cup – the winners getting into the semi-final. Revie and all the Leeds lads agreed: the Tottenham Cup tie was the perfect game to launch the pre-match routine.

On the Friday before Leeds played Tottenham in the FA Cup, I came to ask Revie a favour. Before I could get a word in, Revie started speaking his mind about the upcoming match: 'He knows how to win cups . . . he knows how to win cups. Nicholson has three FA Cups and European and League Cups and that's some collection. A cup tie's a one-off. It's no good saying "it wasn't our day"; it has to be your day or you're out. A drawn game has never won a cup tie. You have to go out and attack. You have to win. That's why Nicholson has been so successful. That's why he has so many cups. His Tottenham teams always go out to attack. That's Nicholson's big strength in cup ties. That's his ace card. He's not afraid to lose. Nicholson's a very tactically astute manager and a great coach. But first and foremost, the man's a winner.' Revie then clenched his right fist, held it up and shook it, adding, 'But not tomorrow.'

Not too confidently, I asked Revie the favour. 'Would you mind if I went to the Queens Hotel this evening to see the Tottenham team and my friends Pat Jennings and Steve Perryman?'

I was sure Revie would say no.

'Go,' came back Revie. 'But don't talk about the Leeds players or tomorrow's pre-match promotion. Not even a word. And if you should see Nicholson, nod and leave. Remember, he's football's best listener,' warned Revie.

I went to the Queens Hotel and in the foyer I saw Nicholson, but only his back view. I hurried past into the lounge and wished Jennings and Perryman luck. Then we talked about teams and players promoting themselves on television.

'Nicholson would never agree to anything like that,' they both said.

Jennings and Perryman were right, but this was not the time to agree and tell them Nicholson's part in why I was with Leeds. It was my cue to leave. It was not until January 2000 that the Nicholson role in the Leeds pre-match promotion was told: first by the award-winning journalist James Brown in the *Leeds, Leeds, Leeds* magazine, and then by Tim Lovejoy and Helen Chamberlain on Sky Sports' *Soccer AM* programme.

In white tracksuit tops with their names on the back and with their numbered stocking tabs hanging on the outside of their socks, the Leeds team led by Les Cocker ran out 15 minutes before three o'clock, split into four and performed their warm-up exercises in the four corners of the field. The crowd went wild, the roar was deafening and I was told Nicholson, on hearing the noise, thought his watch was slow and had come out of the Spurs dressing-room to see what was happening.

That afternoon, Leeds were an irresistible force. With fast-flowing, skilful, attacking football, they beat Tottenham 2–1. Nicholson, as always, was gracious in defeat and admitted Leeds were by far the better team. Revie said the first 20 minutes of football Leeds played was the best he had seen in his life.

Leeds went on to beat Arsenal 1–0 to win the FA Cup for the first time in their history. Allan Clarke had kept his promise. He told me the night before the final that he would score, and he did. If there had been a trophy for the 'Mr Nice Guy' of football, Clarke would have won it every year. Big Jack Charlton gave me one of his signed Wembley stocking tabs and Don Revie walked over and insisted I take, as a permanent reminder of my part in the Leeds success, his FA paper knife, the decorative handle of which had on it the FA Cup and the words, 'To mark the Centenary of the FA Cup Competition 1872–1972'.

'Thanks, Don,' I said.

'No, thank Nicholson,' came back Revie. 'It was his idea you came to Leeds.'

But the man who set it all up, Terry Cooper, who I value dearly as a friend, cruelly missed out. He broke his leg against Stoke and, for me, that took the edge off the Leeds Wembley triumph.

It was at the Holiday Inn, Heathrow, that I next met up with Revie, who had, by then, become the England manager. We were discussing a set of international football cards which featured Ray Clemence, Colin Todd, Gerry Francis and Mick Channon. True to form, Revie blew me away with his clinical and detailed analysis on why he picked these players for his England squads. The tape was a classic. I still have it.

Whenever I was in Revie's company, I always grabbed the opportunity to talk about Tottenham. This was no exception. 'Nicholson and Blanchflower worked as a team. Do you think you and Nicholson could have worked as a team?' I asked Revie.

He laughed: 'I've never given that a thought, but I could definitely have worked with Blanchflower. He had such an inventive football brain. It would have to be the three of us. Nicholson is an idealist: he would settle for nothing less than the beautiful game. I'm a realist: I would be prepared to compromise and come up with a balance that both Nicholson and Blanchflower would be happy with. Blanchflower, the romantic with his head in the clouds, would dream up the most wonderful football tactics and systems.'

Revie went on, warming to the task: 'There would be no problem with the colour of the shirt: both Leeds and Tottenham play in white, and so did Blanchflower at Spurs. As for the change of shirt, I am sure Blanchflower would have insisted on a shade of Irish green. I always thought the Tottenham side needed a bit of the Leeds steel. If I went too heavy, Nicholson would be there to put the brake on. We'd spend hours working on formations, systems and tactics. We would play fast, attacking football. We would turn football on its head, and the fans would love it, I'm sure of that.'

We were both laughing when I left.

The last time I spoke to Revie was prompted by a phone call from Johnny Giles, the former Leeds great. He told me that Revie was very ill and gave me his telephone number and suggested I phoned him. I did, the moment he put the phone down. It was great to hear Revie's voice again and his infectious laugh. We talked about our time together at Leeds and he finished up saying, 'Have you still got the '72 Wembley paper knife?'

I confirmed I had.

'Good,' he said, and added, 'If you do decide one day to part with it, give it to one of the Leeds lads. Keep it in the family.'

That summed up Don Revie. He loved every one of his Leeds team like sons.

I saw Nicholson again when I went down to Tottenham to talk to Alan Gilzean. We had agreed to work together on a World Cup promotional heading-practice chart for Wm Macdonald & Sons. I always found it impossible to go down to Tottenham without bumping into Nicholson, and as I waited for Gilzean, he stepped into the picture.

'What are you down here for?' Nicholson was always straight to the point.

'I've come to see Alan Gilzean about a World Cup heading chart. Did he tell you about it?'

'You'll have to wait a bit,' Nicholson replied. 'He's still changing.' Then, as he turned to leave, he said, 'You didn't tell me about the exercise-routine idea.'

I was surprised Nicholson had brought up Leeds. I had decided if I met him, it was the one subject I would steer well clear of. 'I didn't have it then,' I said. 'It wasn't until I saw Leeds training that I came up with it.'

Nicholson came back, 'You've seen Tottenham training.'

I agreed, 'I know. I've also seen Arsenal, Chelsea and West Ham, but Leeds – they were something else. They were super fit, football gymnasts, Olympic standard, military precision – unbelievable!'

Nicholson nodded: 'We all do it now. All the teams come out early and warm up on the pitch. The stocking tabs, they'll be forgotten, but the warm-up routines are here to stay. You've made your mark in football.'

A compliment from Nicholson! I took a step forward. I wanted to be within arm's reach as I believed my next question could earn me a pat on the back. 'Bill,' I said, 'if I had come to you with the exercise-routines idea, would you have said yes?'

Nicholson did put his hand on my shoulder. Then he looked me straight in the eye and said, 'No,' and walked away.

Trevillion on Nicholson:
a 50-year relationship

The house in which I was born was 109 Love Lane, Tottenham. It was no more than a corner kick from the Tottenham Hotspur football ground. I went to the St Francis De Sales School, which was even nearer: less than a penalty kick away from the ground. In January 1947 – the first season of league football after the Second World War – I had slipped out of school and was standing outside the Tottenham football ground holding a newspaper cutting of the Tottenham Hotspur football team.

The back row of the team picture read: G. Hardy [late trainer – George Hardy, the Tottenham coach and trainer, had passed away that week, days before Tottenham's match against West Bromwich Albion]; G. Ludford; A. Willis; E. Ditchburn; V. Buckingham; R. Burgess; S. Tickridge. The front row was: C. Whitchurch, L. Bennett, G. Foreman, J. Hulme (manager), L. Stevens, L. Medley, W. Nicholson.

'You're too late, son. They've all gone.'

I looked across to the man leaning against the wall outside the Spurs gates. I turned to leave, when the voice called out again.

'Hold on, son. There's Bill Nicholson – get his autograph. He'll sign. Nicholson always signs.'

I didn't hesitate. I ran straight up to Nicholson and handed him the newspaper cutting. Nicholson took it, signed and, without a word, gave it straight back to me. I wasn't happy. Nicholson had signed his name: 'W. Nicholson'. It didn't look right. I wanted: 'B. Nicholson'.

The look of disappointment on my face had Nicholson asking, 'What's wrong? Did you think I was someone else? Some other player?'

I shook my head. 'No,' I replied. 'I've seen you play. I know you're Bill Nicholson, but you've signed with a "W". You're Bill Nicholson; you should have signed with a "B".'

'My name's "William". I always sign with a "W".' He then looked at me and was very firm when he said, 'No matter how many times you ask me for my autograph, I will always sign it "W. Nicholson".' With that, he walked away.

'Thank you, Mr Nicholson,' I called out.

Nicholson turned, smiled and said, 'Call me Bill!'

At that moment, I was the proudest boy in Tottenham. The Spurs goalkeeper, Ted Ditchburn, was my hero, but I now believed Nicholson was my *friend*. He wanted me to call him 'Bill'. I guarded that newspaper cutting of the Tottenham Hotspur team with my life. I still have it, and 'W. Nicholson' in blue ink is the only signature on it.

My next vivid memory of Nicholson was thanks to Arthur Rowe, the manager of the record-breaking Tottenham push-and-run side. It was just before the start of the 1954–55 season. Arthur Rowe had invited me into his office to help me complete a drawing of him for the front cover of the Tottenham *Lilywhite* magazine .

'Is this by Royal appointment?' laughed Arthur, as I sat down. He was referring to a letter I had received from Buckingham Palace in which his Royal Highness, the Duke of Edinburgh, believed my sketch of him was 'a very good piece of work'.

I laughed and, as I got busy with my pencil, we talked about Tottenham and the players.

'You drew Charlie Withers on the front page of the *Lilywhite* last year,' reminded Rowe.

'You're right,' I said. 'That was because you pulled off a stroke of unbelievable genius when you played Withers on the wing in the cup tie against Preston. He scored both goals and with him again on the wing, we won the replay.'

SUPPORTERS' NEWS

By RAY MARLER

('Sporting Record' is the official organ of the National Federation of Football Supporters' Clubs)

LESLIE DAVIS, the National Federation General Secretary, tells me hundreds of soccer supporters, from all over the country, will be at Harringay in two weeks time for the special evening at Tom Arnold's Circus, arranged by the Federation.

For this occasion, each club attendi... inviting two of its own players as guests of the evening, which will turn out a real gala night fo... the terrace HELP NOT HINDE...

JOHN BULL

CROSSWORD No. 8...

Across—

1. It's easier to do this in the ...ark —BUNGLE. Burgling is don... night—by day the offence is called housebreaking.

4. It's wise to distrust deep this— Sea, SET, sex. A deep set of subtle, untrustworthy people preferred.

5. If unaccustomed to this on river, it's apt to make one rather apprehensive—SHELL. You may fear it will overturn at any moment. The swell would have to be very violent to cause apprehension.

6. Young children fairly often do...

Honour for Paul Trevillion, talented cartoonist of Lilywhite, magazine of **Spurs Supporters' Club**, is acceptance by The Duke of Edinburgh of a cartoon of him, drawn by Trevillion.

Latest issue of the magazi... ...tion of the outst... match pictures so far this season, and with its various features (Ted Ditchburn is among the contributors), there's good reading.

I note one article mentions the affinity between football and table tennis, and recalls how Victor Barna, biggest table tennis name ever, and himself a former junior international in Hungary, trains with Chelsea players for fitness, while Johnny Leach, another English world champion turns out...

Supporters have built a te... room, costing over £400, and ea... first team home match ente... ...m as guests, six members of t... ...siting team's supporters' club. great work of theirs is the spec... ...ine they've installed from Ea... End Park to Dunfermline a... W.F. Hospital; commentaries a... given on all home matches. T... parent club directors and su... porters have a monthly meetin... which helps to mutual und... standing.

Dancing date for **Arsenal Foo... ball Supporters' Club** is their ... Valentine's night Dance, at Fi... bury Town Hall, on Saturd... February 14.

Features of particular inter...

Sporting Record, 1952

Charlie Withers was the Spurs left-back who shared the position with Arthur Willis, and Arthur Rowe surprised just about everyone by picking left-back Withers to play on the left-wing. Arthur's reply came as a big surprise.

'That wasn't my idea,' admitted Rowe. 'It was Nicholson's. He believed we had the perfect opportunity. Remember we didn't have our regular outside-left, Les Medley, to play an extra defender in a free role to help put the brake on Tom Finney. It worked. The two goals Withers scored were an unexpected bonus. No, I must be fair, all the credit for that bit of tactical "genius", as you call it, goes to Nicholson.'

Rowe continued, as I put the finishing touches to the drawing: 'Nicholson has all the qualities to be a great coach. That's what he will finish up doing at Tottenham.'

The drawing was finished. 'Do you mean,' I asked Arthur, 'that Nicholson will soon stop playing?'

'Yes,' replied Arthur. 'Sooner rather than later. Then I believe he will take up coaching duties at Tottenham.'

I left Arthur Rowe's office feeling very sad that Nicholson's playing

THE *Lilywhite*

THE OFFICIAL ORGAN OF THE SPURS SUPPORTERS CLUB

Vol. 3 No. 7   *Affiliated to the National Federation of Supporters Clubs*   Price **6d.**

SPECIAL ARTICLE

How we WON THE CUP in 1921

CHARLIE WITHERS

P. TREVILLION

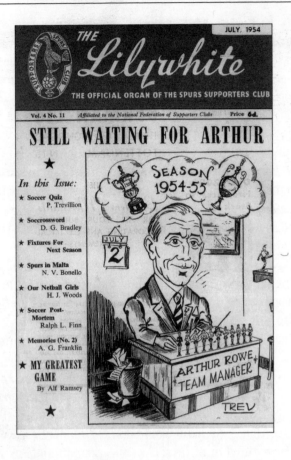

days were coming to an end, but I was happy with the thought he would at least stay on at Tottenham, even if only as a coach!

Arthur Rowe was pleased with his drawing on the front cover of *Lilywhite*, and he was kind enough to encourage me to continue with my art.

I acted on Rowe's advice and continued with my drawings in the Tottenham *Lilywhite* magazine, and a full-page drawing of Nicholson brought about another Bill Nicholson memorable moment.

'The name's Bill, not Billy,' said Nicholson, and, as always, I knew he was acknowledging in his usual blunt way the drawing published in the *Lilywhite* in which I had written 'Billy Nicholson' under my drawing with the caption: 'Coach but no driver!' It went on:

Billy Nicholson, who has been appointed coach to Spurs' Spurlets, will probably not be seen in the Tottenham colours this season. But if Bill can enthuse into the youngsters the same 90-minute endeavour and go-ahead, never-say-die spirit which always characterised his own play, then the Spurs will have good reason for satisfaction.

Both Bill and I were standing in the Spurs car park.

'What about skill?' said Nicholson. 'You never mentioned skill. That's what Tottenham's all about: skilful players and skilful football. Always remember that, when you next do one of your drawings.'

I smiled, and then, fishing for a compliment, I said, 'Did you like your drawing, Bill?'

He walked away, muttering, 'Well, at least it looked a bit like me.'

That was par for the course. I would have to wait a lot longer, many years in fact, before I was to receive my much sought-after word of praise from Bill. And as for Bill actually calling me by my name, or even just my surname, it never happened! To Bill, I was the man with no name.

'I hope you look good in black.' It was Nicholson again, and this time he was none too happy. It was January 1960, and I had screamed from the rooftops in the *Tottenham Weekly Herald* under the heading 'Double Talk' that Tottenham would do the Double. I was so sure, I had sketched in a drawing of myself in the cartoon and insisted that if Spurs failed to do the Double, I would wear a black tie for the next 12 months. Tottenham's Dave Mackay, due to a boil on his knee, missed the third-round home tie at Tottenham, and Blackburn, the visitors, upset the odds and won 3–1. Spurs were out of the Cup and the Double dream was over even before it had begun, and this was the reason for a very unhappy Bill Nicholson standing in front of me.

'Spurs will do it next season, Bill,' I said. But he wasn't listening.

'You make sure,' said Nicholson, 'you wear a black tie for a year and remember – it was way back in 1897 when the Double was last done. So be a bit more responsible when you do your *Herald* cartoons. Take your football a bit more seriously and don't forget to wear the black tie.'

Nicholson, as usual, walked off.

COACH BUT NO DRIVER !

BILLY NICHOLSON, who has been appointed coach to 'Spurs' Spurlets, will probably not be seen in the Tottenham colours this season. But if Bill can enthuse into the youngsters the same 90 minute endeavour and go-ahead, never-say-die spirit which always characterised his own play; then the 'Spurs will have good reason for satisfaction.

Billy Nicholson

Lilywhite magazine, 1954

Tottenham Weekly Herald, 1960

'I still think you'll win the Double next year,' I called out, but Nicholson did not respond. He kept on walking.

Not only did I wear a black tie, everything else I wore was black, and, despite Tottenham's Double success the following year, I've kept that look from that day to this. Even in the very last picture I had taken with Nicholson, in 1993, I was still wearing all black – it became a sort of trademark!

In 1974, Wm Macdonald & Sons of Isleworth launched a World Cup promotion with their 'Bandit' and 'Munchmallow' biscuits, in conjunction with McVitie's 'Sports' biscuits. Scotland was the only British team that had qualified for the finals and they wanted a Scottish player to drive a campaign for a World Cup header-training wall chart.

Thanks to the Arsenal goalkeeper, Bob Wilson, whom I had worked with on a piece for the *Sunday People* entitled 'Gilly Knows the Angles', with Wilson explaining just why Tottenham's Alan Gilzean was so masterful in the air, I was able to convince Wm Macdonald & Sons to use Alan Gilzean for the World Cup headers chart.

Gilzean was up for it and between us we produced a magnificent 31 in. x 46 in. full-colour wall chart showing all the heading skills. But just before the launch, Wm Macdonald & Sons decided they would like in writing that Bill Nicholson had given permission for Alan Gilzean to go ahead with this promotion.

I went down to Tottenham and asked Gilzean if he could get a letter to this effect from Bill Nicholson. Gilzean, who was a very likeable man and easy to work with, said it wasn't necessary. He said he had told Nicholson he was doing the chart and he was quite happy about it.

I went back to Wm Macdonald & Sons and told them that Nicholson had given Gilzean his word that he could go ahead and it wasn't necessary to have it in writing: Nicholson was a man of his word. Wm Macdonald & Sons were not happy with this and insisted that they had Bill Nicholson's confirmation in writing. So I went to see Bill. As always, it was a short conversation.

'I'm too busy to write a letter. I've told Gilzean it's all right by me for him to do the heading chart and that's good enough.'

When I went back to Wm Macdonald & Sons, I expected trouble, but they had phoned around. I never found out whom they had spoken to, but apparently they had it on good authority that when Bill Nicholson

Gilly knows the angles

Alan Gilzean scored two and made the other two of Tottenham's four goals that knocked Carlisle out of the Cup after a replay.
This week Roy Tunks, Rotherham's goalkeeper, faces the Gilly goal threat.
A daunting task, but one that hasn't worried Arsenal's 'keeper, Bob Wilson —Tottenham have squeezed only one goal past him in their last three meetings. Now Wilson talks us through Gilzean's game.

Gilzean's not a power header of a ball—not like Ron and Wyn Davies. When they head a ball it really goes. Even so, I'd rather face these two than Gilly. With them, you know what to expect, so you're moving fractionally before they hammer it. You're in with a chance. But Gilly is impossible to " read "—and if you're foolish enough to try, it's odds on he'll wrong-foot you. And when a goalkeeper's off-balance, he can be made to look a MUG.

THROW-INS

When Chivers takes a long throw-in down by the corner flag, Gilly's the target man. You'll find him hovering around the penalty spot poised to flick the ball on, glance it down or head at goal himself.

GILZEAN

NEAR-POST DANGER

No matter how impossible the angle, never rule Gilzean out of a goal effort.
Move off your line in anticipation of Gilly heading the ball across the goal and you'll find he's glanced the ball inside the near post.

GILZEAN

I can name no other striker who, with his BACK to goal, is as deadly as Gilzean. With most forwards it's safe to anticipate a straight-forward knock-back and position yourself accordingly.

BACK TO GOAL

KNOCK-BACK

CROSS   SHOT

With Gilly, everything's on-so don't commit yourself too early. WAIT till he shows his hand—then GO.

KNOCK-BACK

CROSS

BACK-HEADER   SIDE-FLICK

TIGHT SITUATIONS
Never underestimate Gilzean, even when he's hopelessly outnumbered with no room to work. With Gilly everything's possible—even the IMPOSSIBLE.

DEVISED AND DRAWN BY TREVILLION

Sunday People, 1972

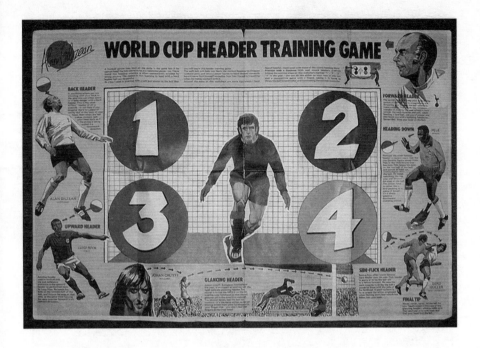

Wm Macdonald & Sons, 1974

Soccer Skills with Gazza, Stanley Paul, 1991

gave his word, it was better than a piece of paper. The promotion went ahead and it was a great success.

My last meeting with Bill Nicholson was in 1993. I had gone down to Tottenham to see Teddy Sheringham in connection with a *Sun* newspaper promotion on football pin badges. Sheringham, who I always believed had the football brain of Les Allen and the scoring skills of Alan Gilzean, was the most underrated player ever to play up-front for Tottenham.

As always, every time I went down to Tottenham I always seemed to bump into Bill Nicholson. In fact, during the 50 years I knew Bill

Striker Skills and Tactics, Stanley Paul, 1991

Nicholson you could count on one hand the number of meetings that were actually planned. I was always down at Tottenham on other business, and somehow he seemed to know I was there. This day was no exception.

I recalled with Bill the good old days of the push-and-run side and the glory days of the Double team and then I asked him if Gascoigne or Lineker would have got into those teams. Bill nodded: 'I would have found a place for them somewhere. They would have been in the squad.'

I had my arm around Bill and we were posing for a photograph, and

223

he said, 'I've seen the Gary Lineker book and the Paul Gascoigne book that you did. Well done!'

For the first time, a word of praise from Bill. I turned and said, 'Can I have that in writing?!'

Bill smiled and replied, 'Forget I said it!' And, with that, he disappeared off into the Tottenham club.

The photograph that was taken that day is my favourite. Bill has the biggest smile I ever saw in all my memories of him, which lit up the great man's face.

A 'well done' from Bill and a big smile on his face: it took 50 years, and, for me, that was my Tottenham Double.

List of Illustrations

Index